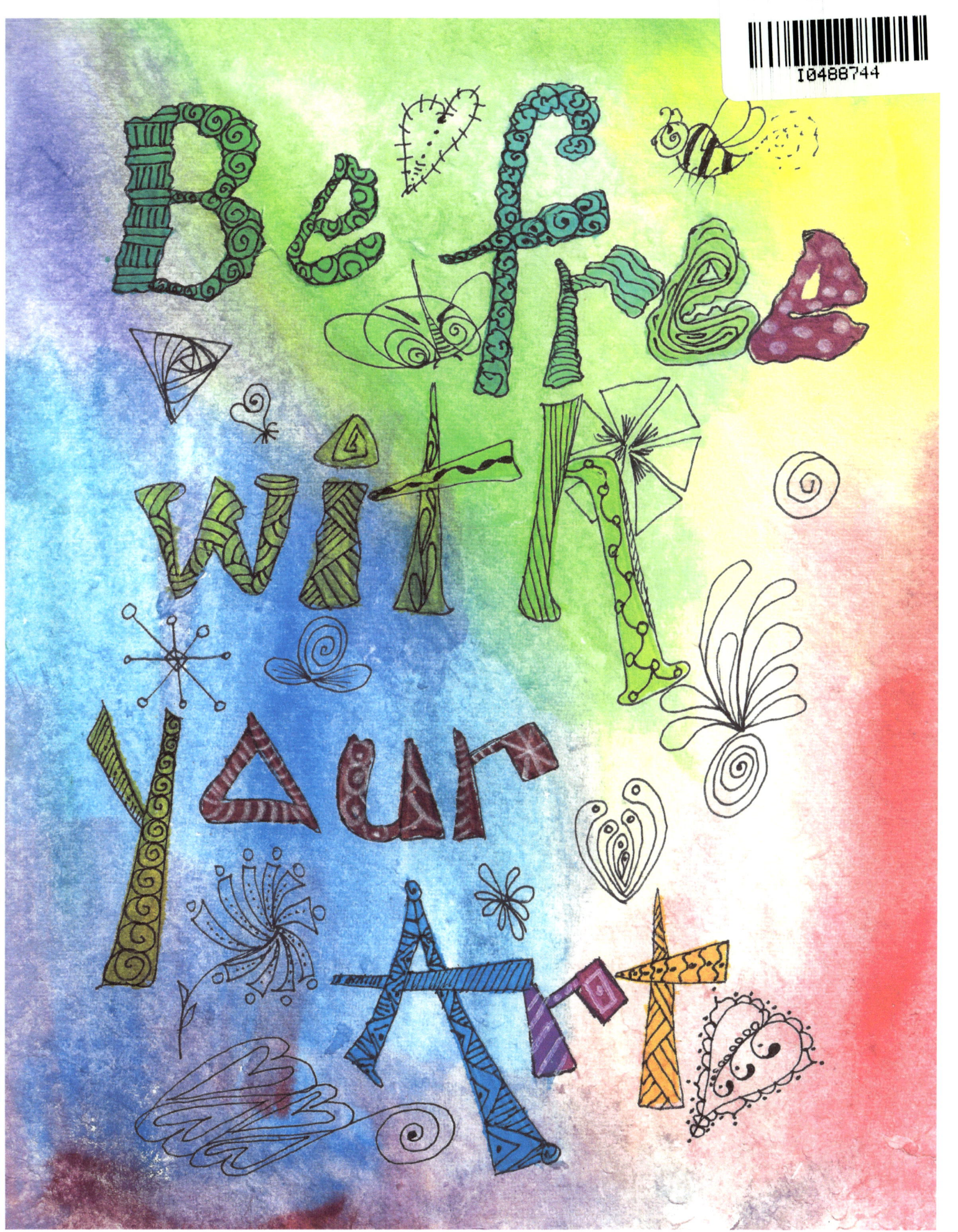

~ Dedication ~
To all my tangling pals and those who so willingly work to help me
be the best Zentangle Teacher that I can be.
I am forever in your debt.
Thank you for your continued support and encouragement.

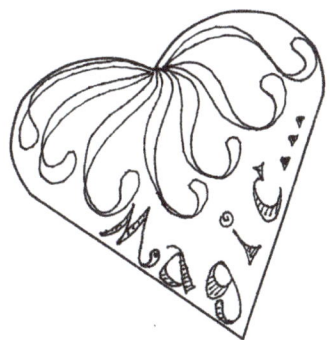

Welcome to
Heart Strings ~ Book 1
of the series

Heart strings sounds so romantic, but truthfully, they are my way of connecting to Zentangle and the other numerous things in my life. Over and over, I find everything around me is connected in some way or another, Nature's balance, if you will.

When you see something wonderful, doesn't it make you smile, and your heart feel good? It does for me. And, when we see something not so good, or experience that, our heart again reacts to it. Our whole body does, but our heart especially.

In this interactive Zentangle® coloring and tangling book, you'll have the chance to create what *you* want and to express what *your* heart feels through this wonderful art form. There's no experience necessary, no mistakes, and only possibilities. Zentangle® allows us to relax long enough to get in touch with our inner selves, to examine how we feel, and to express it with colors and drawing. Don't get me wrong, this isn't art therapy, and I'm not a doctor of any kind. I simply realize how this art form effects me, benefits me, and how it brings me peace in an otherwise zany and crazy world. Our lives are full of *STUFF* that's sometimes good and sometimes not so good. When the not so good comes along, I use the art of tangling to bring calm and tranquility back into the atmosphere.

With *you* in mind, I've made an effort to not only teach you to tangle, but to bring the benefits of this soothing and creative art form to you. I hope you enjoy the book as much as I've enjoyed creating it. You can find me, Jeanne Paglio, on Facebook and on my blog at http://zenoftangling.blogspot.com

I'd enjoy hearing from you!

Jeanne ♥

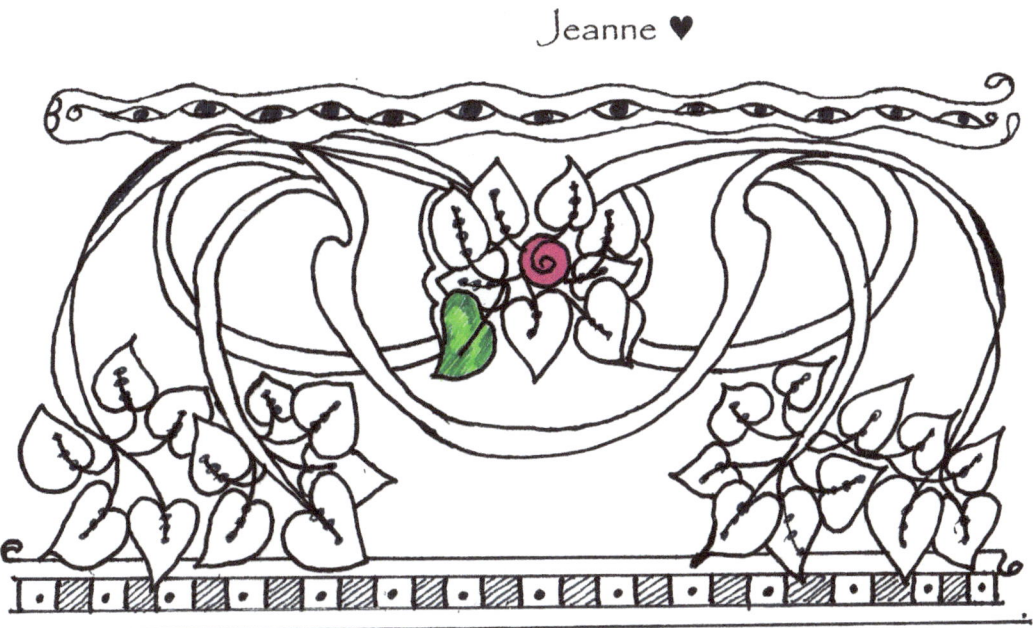

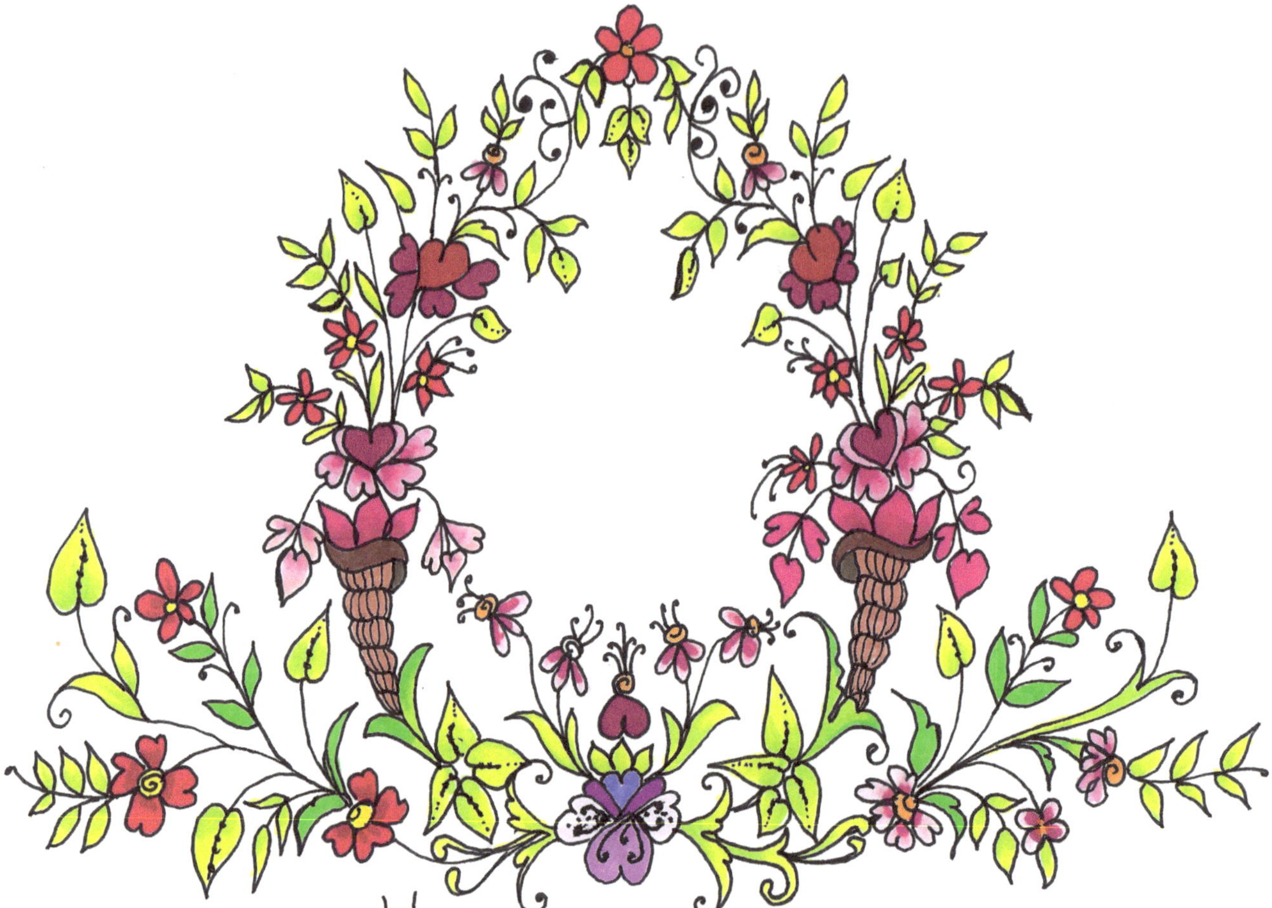

Hearts & flowers

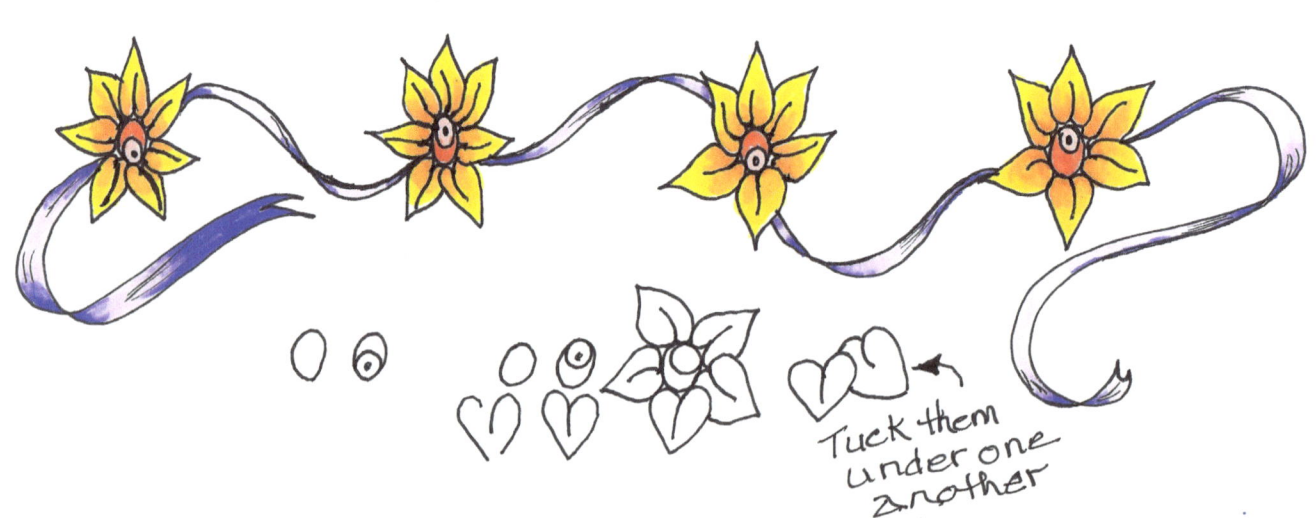

Tuck them
under one
another

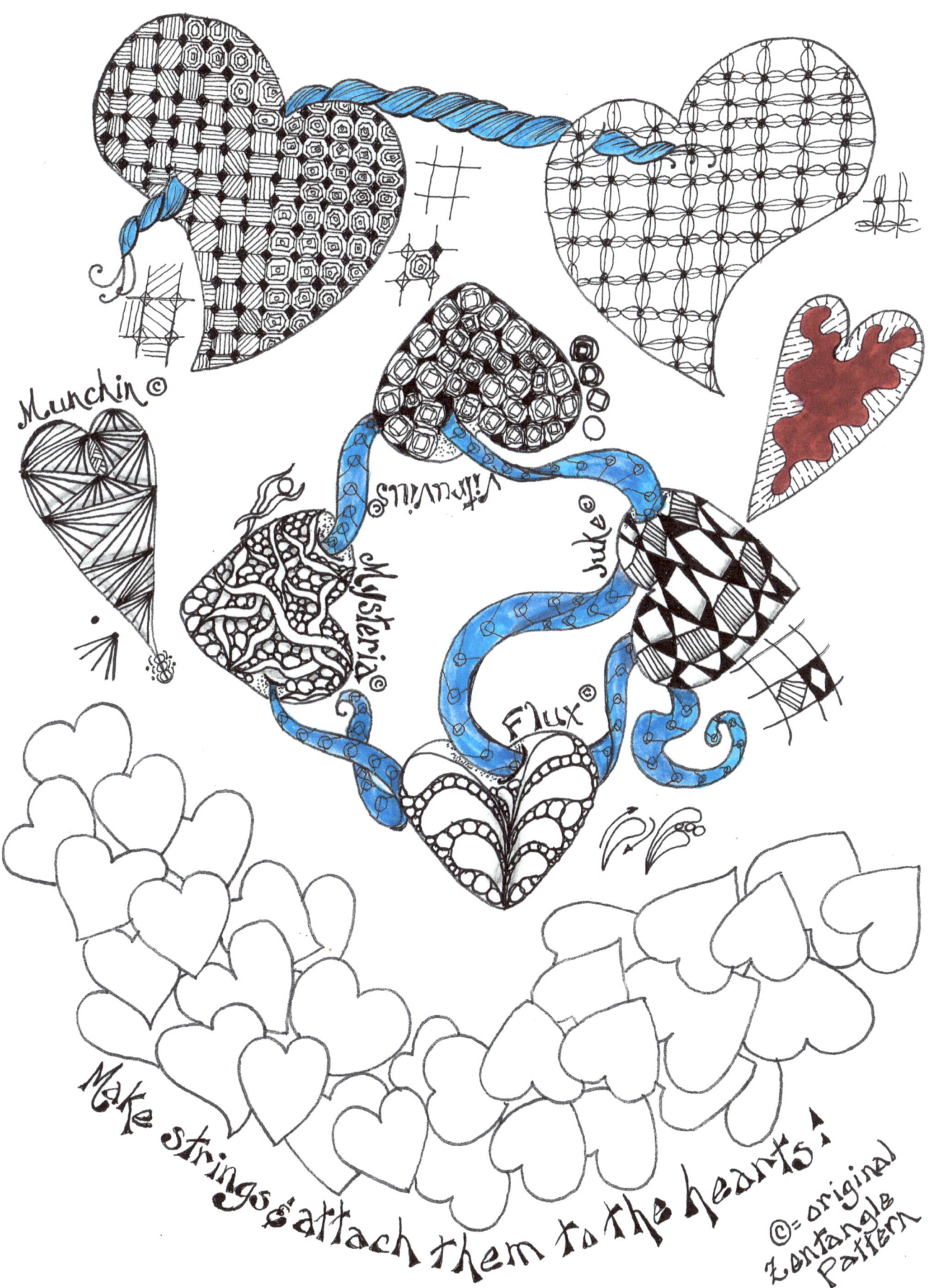

Munchin©

Mysteria©

Vitruvius©

Juke©

Flux©

Make strings & attach them to the hearts!

©= original Zentangle Pattern

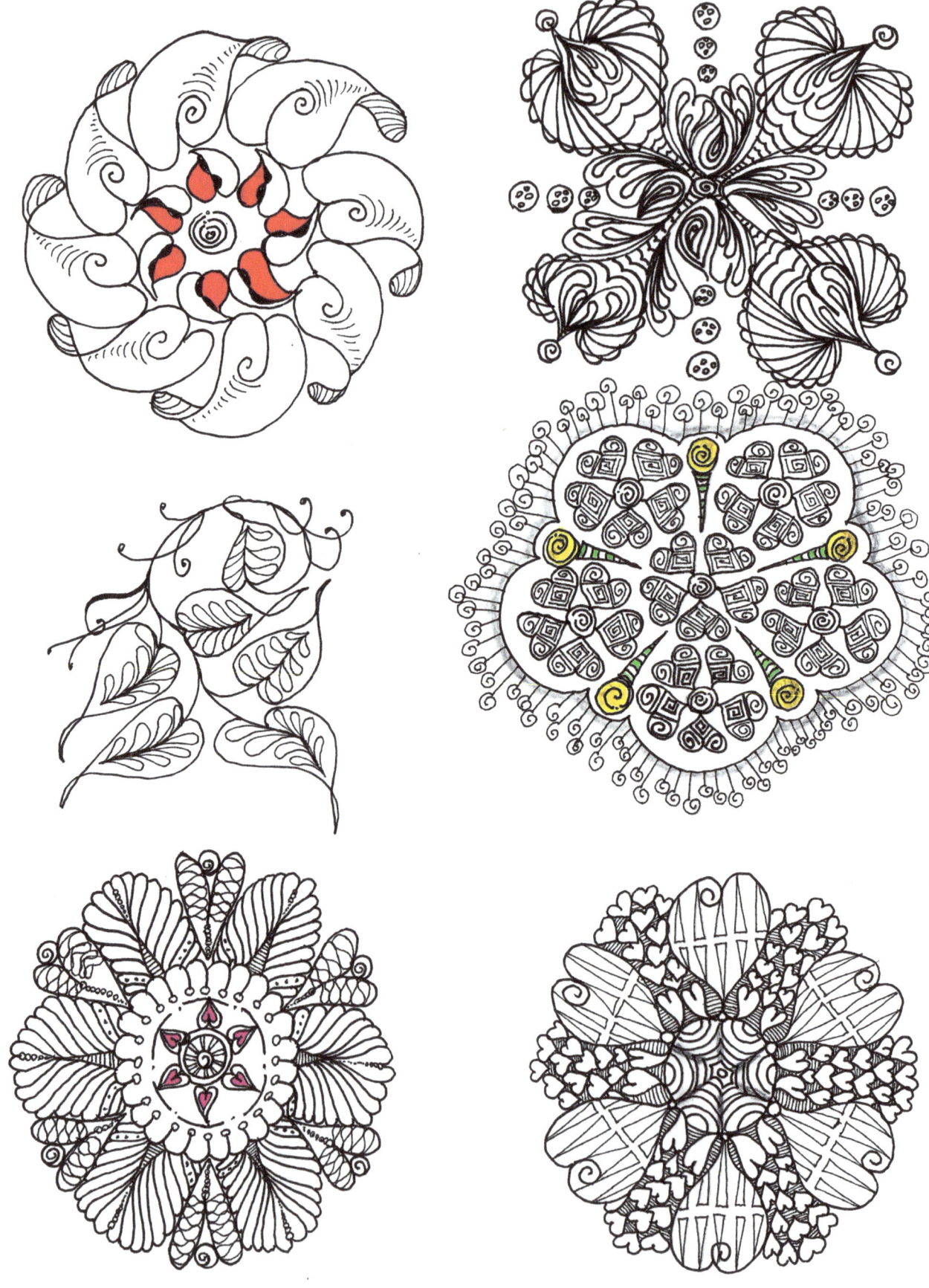

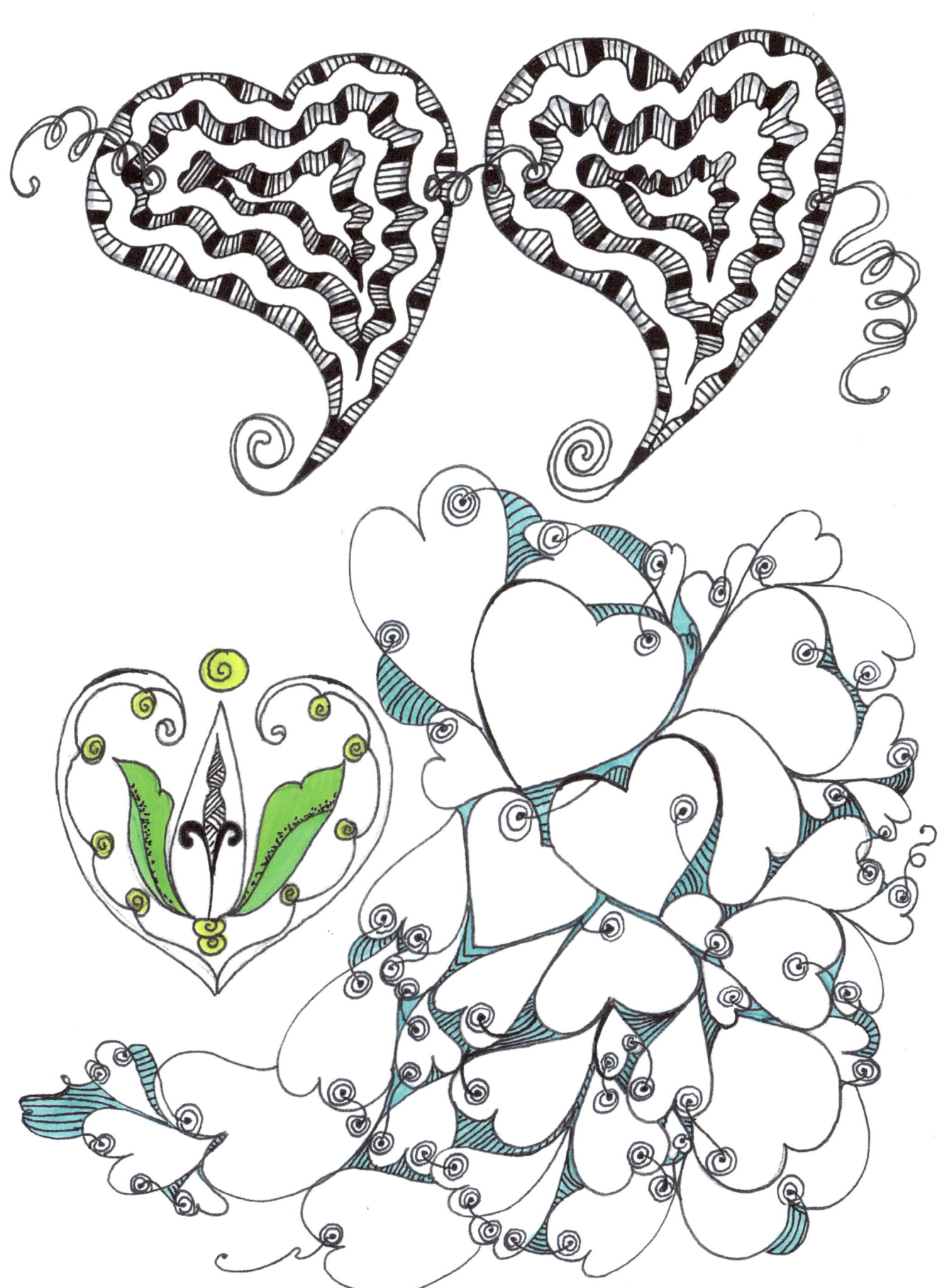

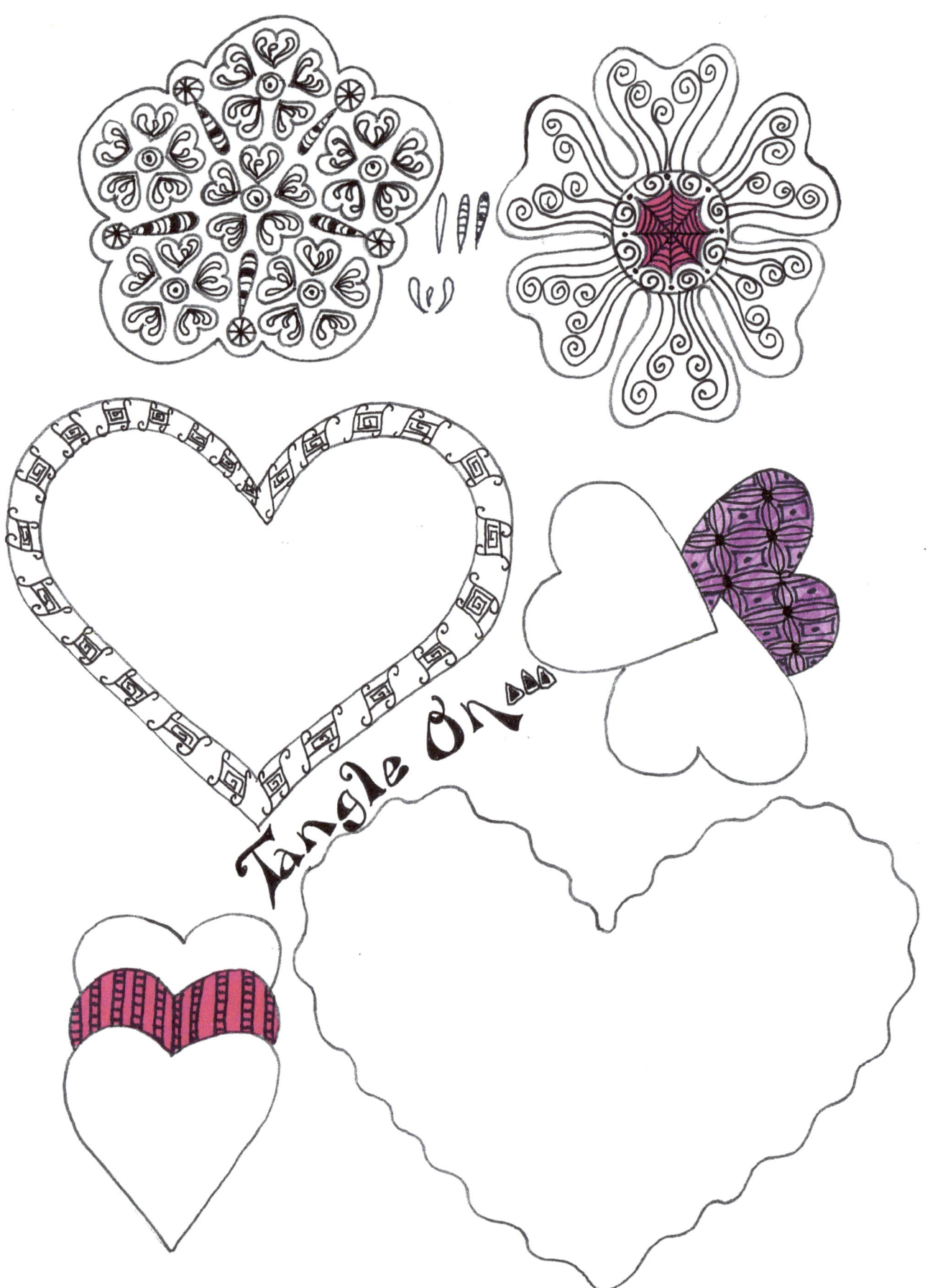

Tangle On

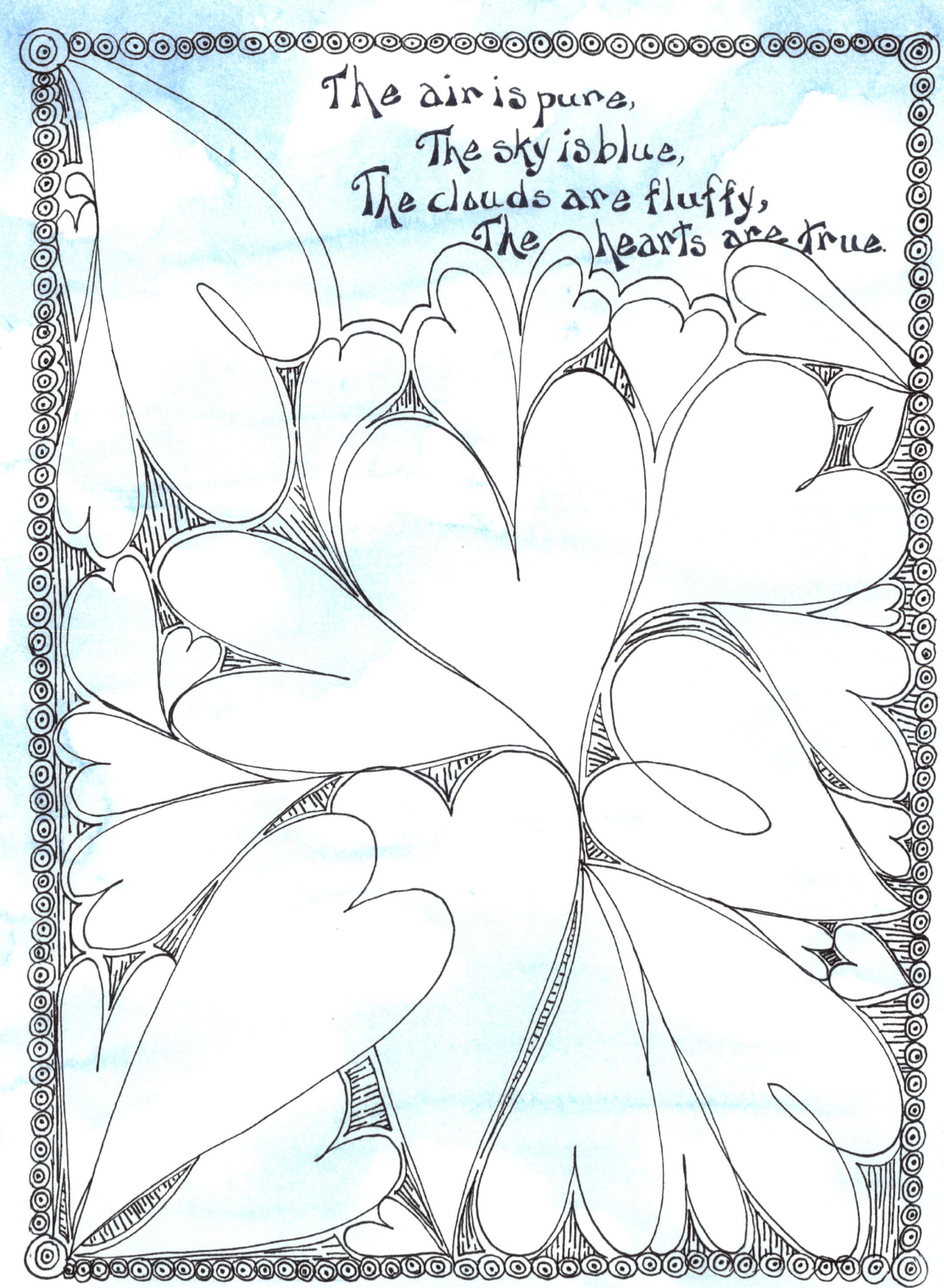

The air is pure,
The sky is blue,
The clouds are fluffy,
The hearts are true.

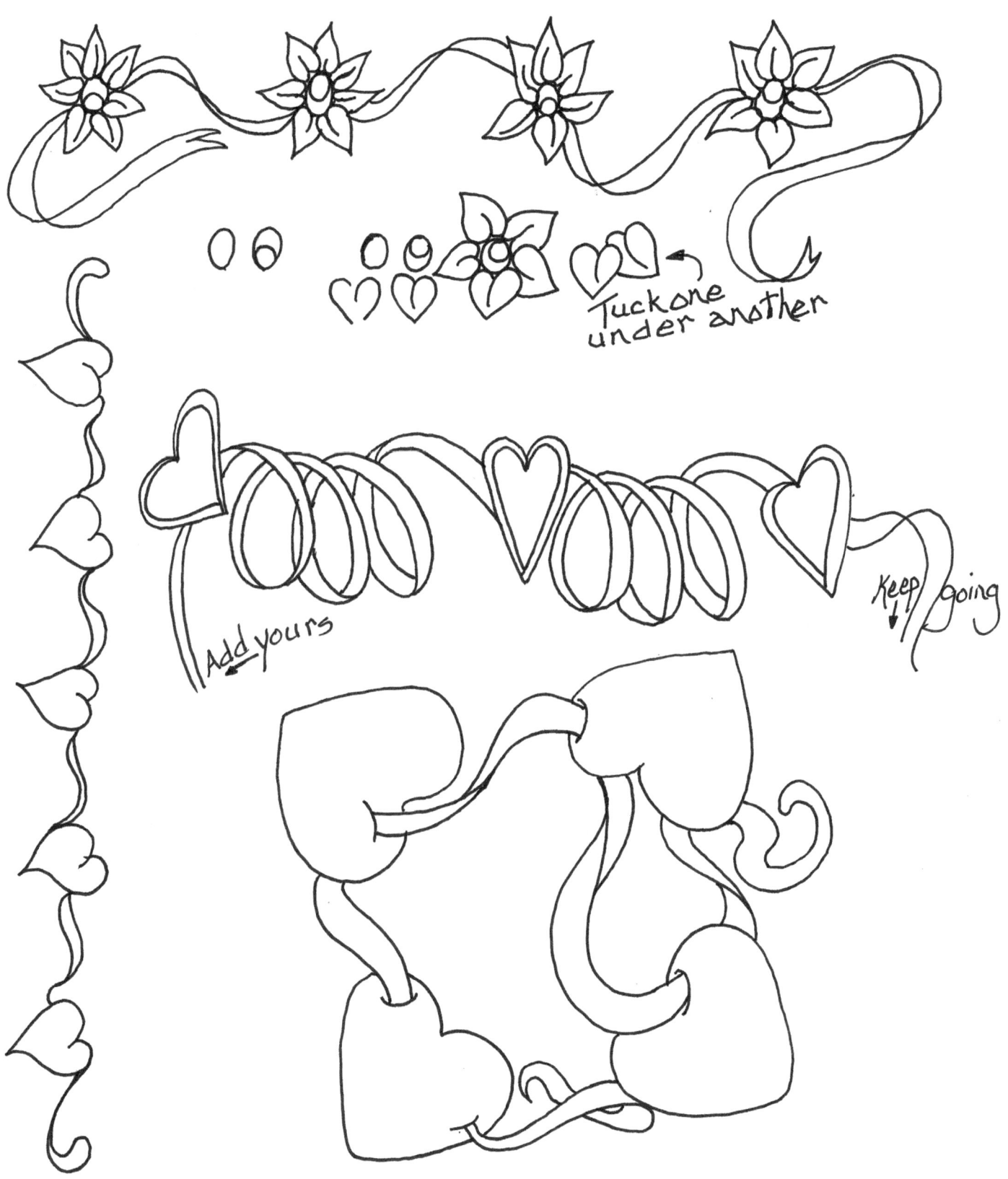

Tuck one under another

Add yours

Keep going

Share your heart string
designs with a friend...

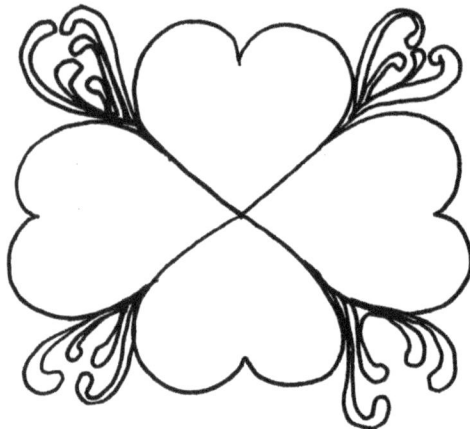

Design your heart
strings here...

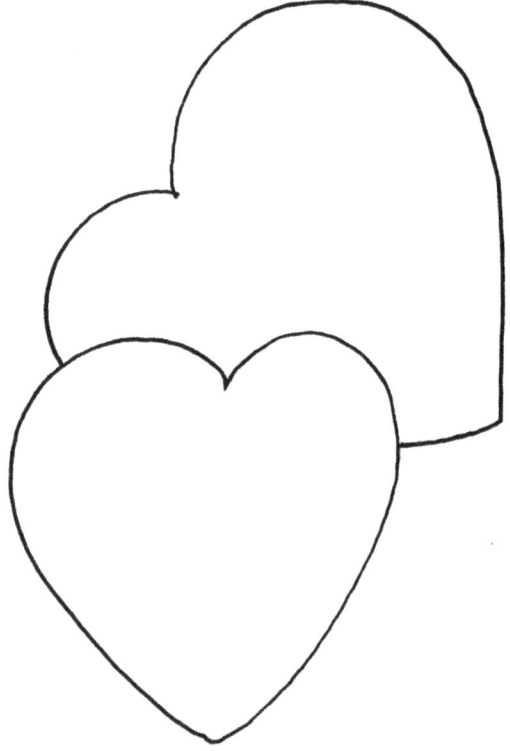

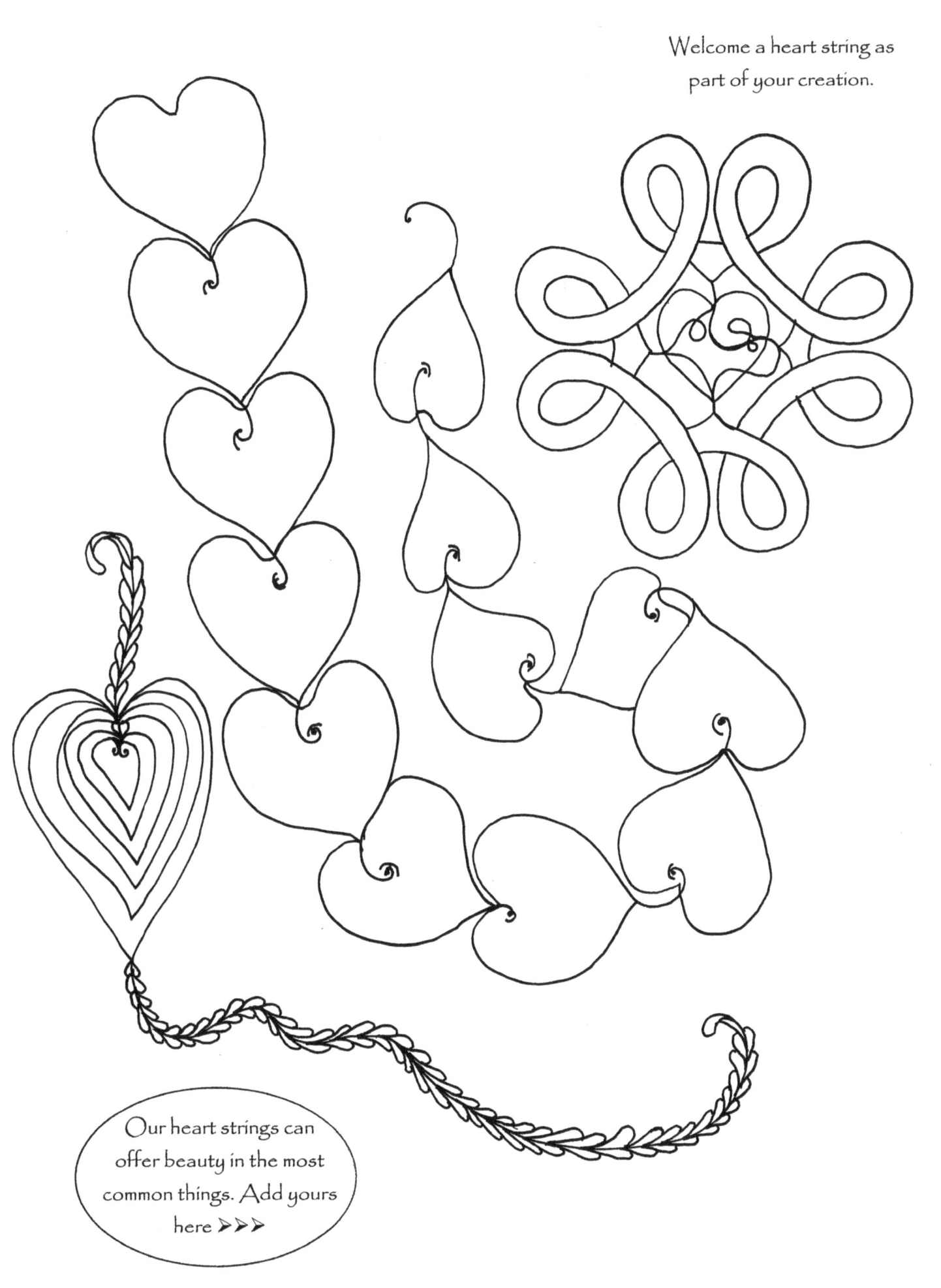

Welcome a heart string as
part of your creation.

Our heart strings can
offer beauty in the most
common things. Add yours
here ▶▶▶

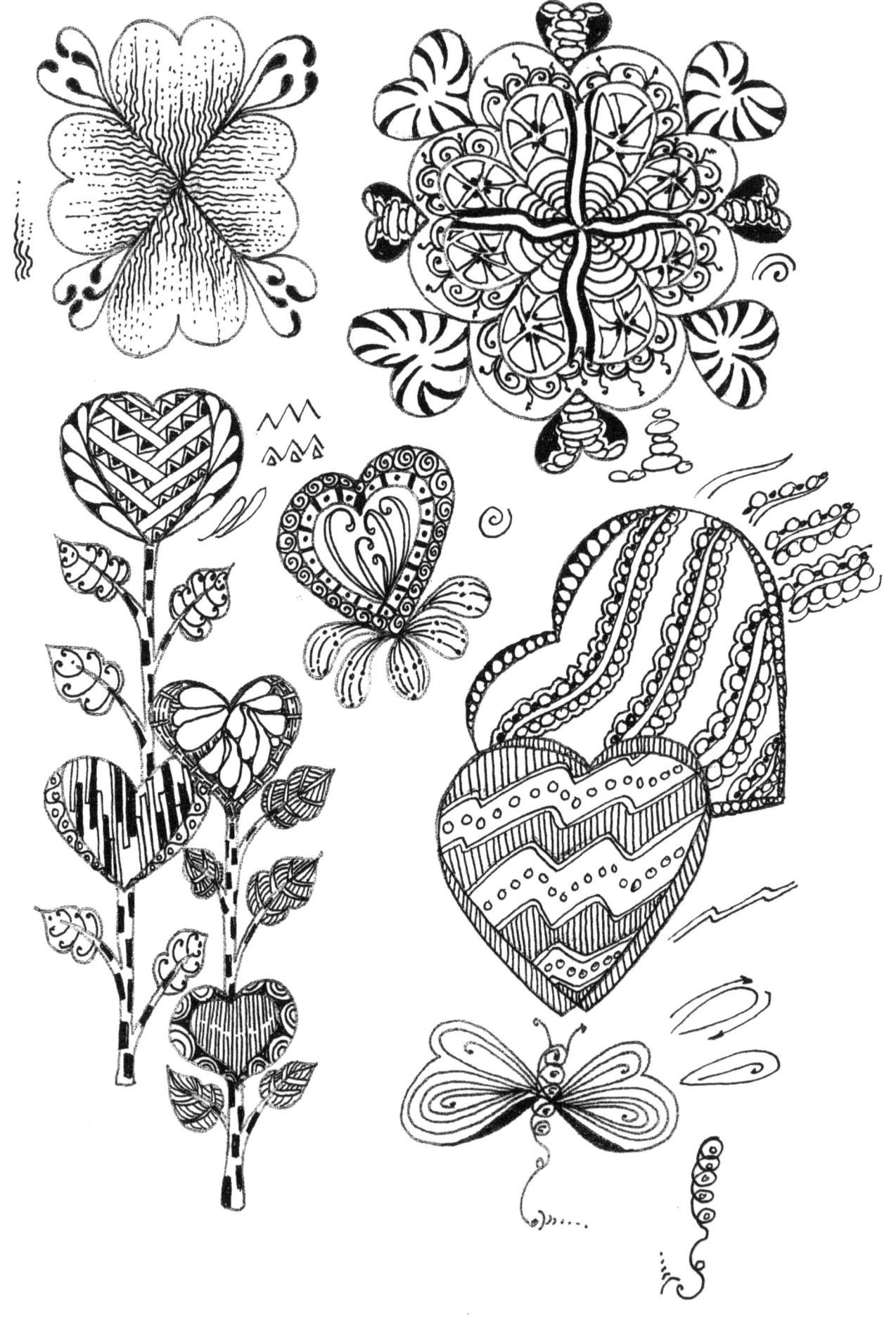

Learn the art of strings and where they can lead. Have fun with them, enjoy the journey!

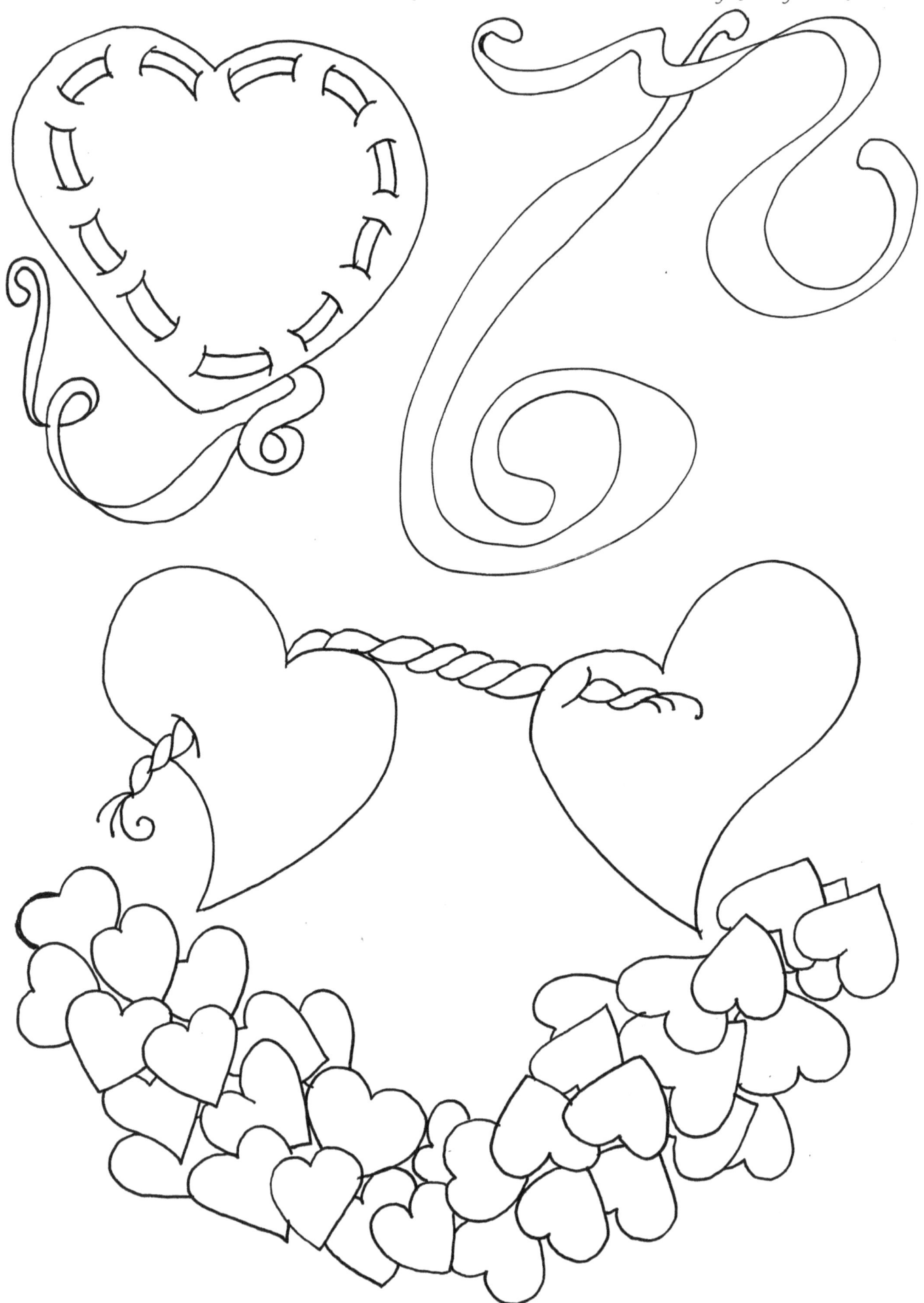

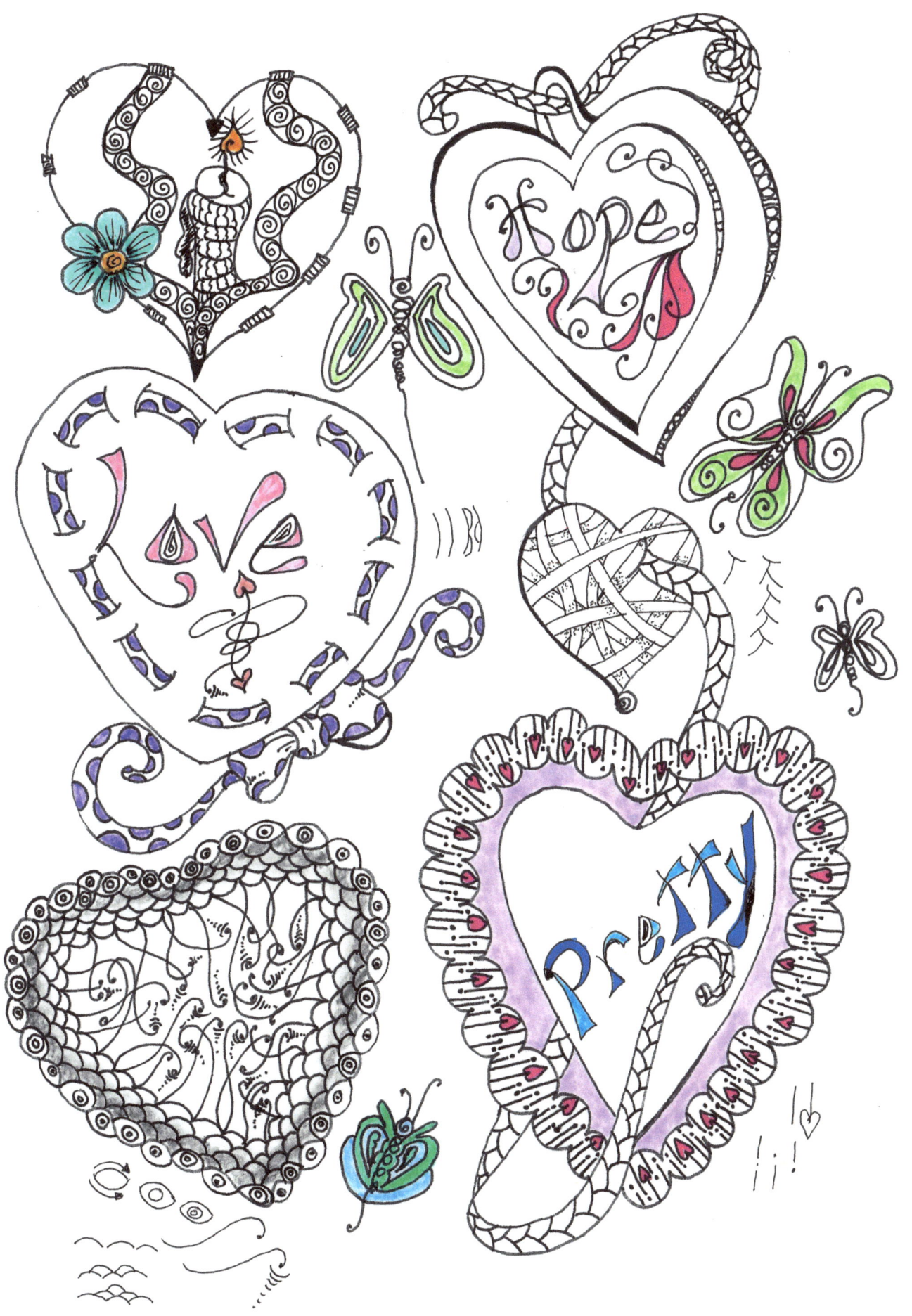

Art Unity

Hugs

Bliss

Soar

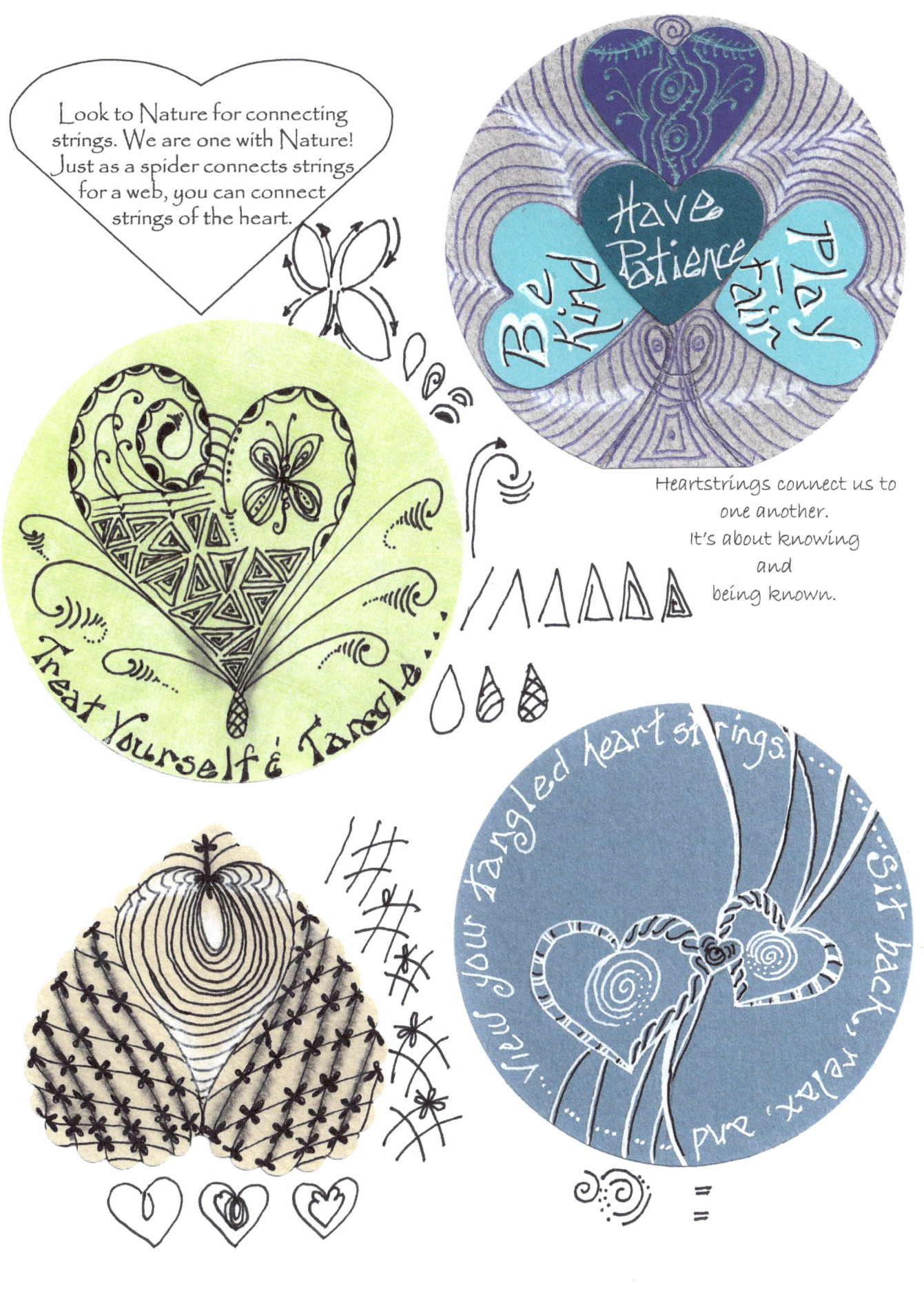

Look to Nature for connecting strings. We are one with Nature! Just as a spider connects strings for a web, you can connect strings of the heart.

Have Patience

Be Kind

Play Fair

Heartstrings connect us to one another. It's about knowing and being known.

Treat Yourself & Tangle . . .

View your tangled heart strings . . . Sit back, relax, and . . .

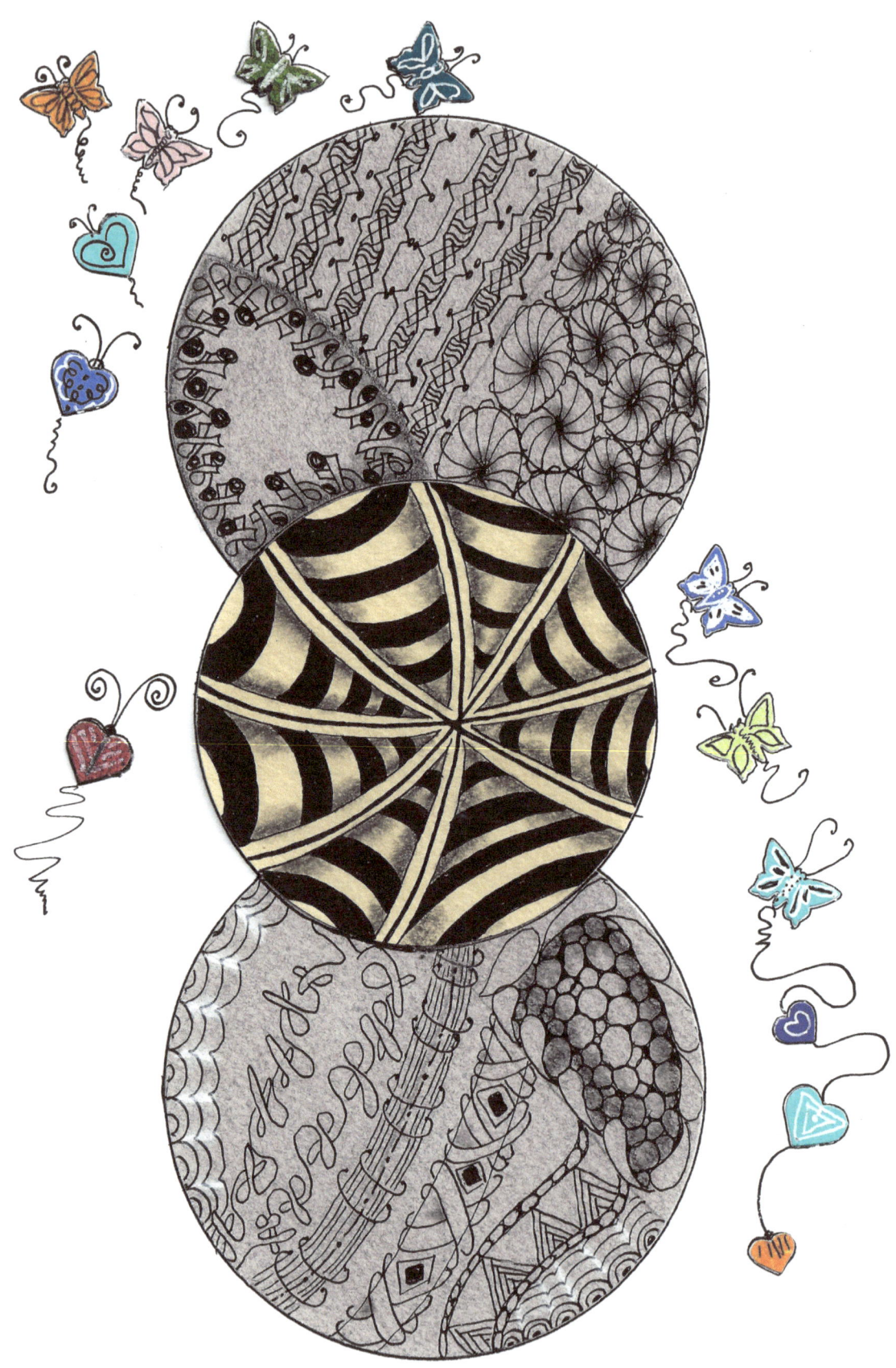

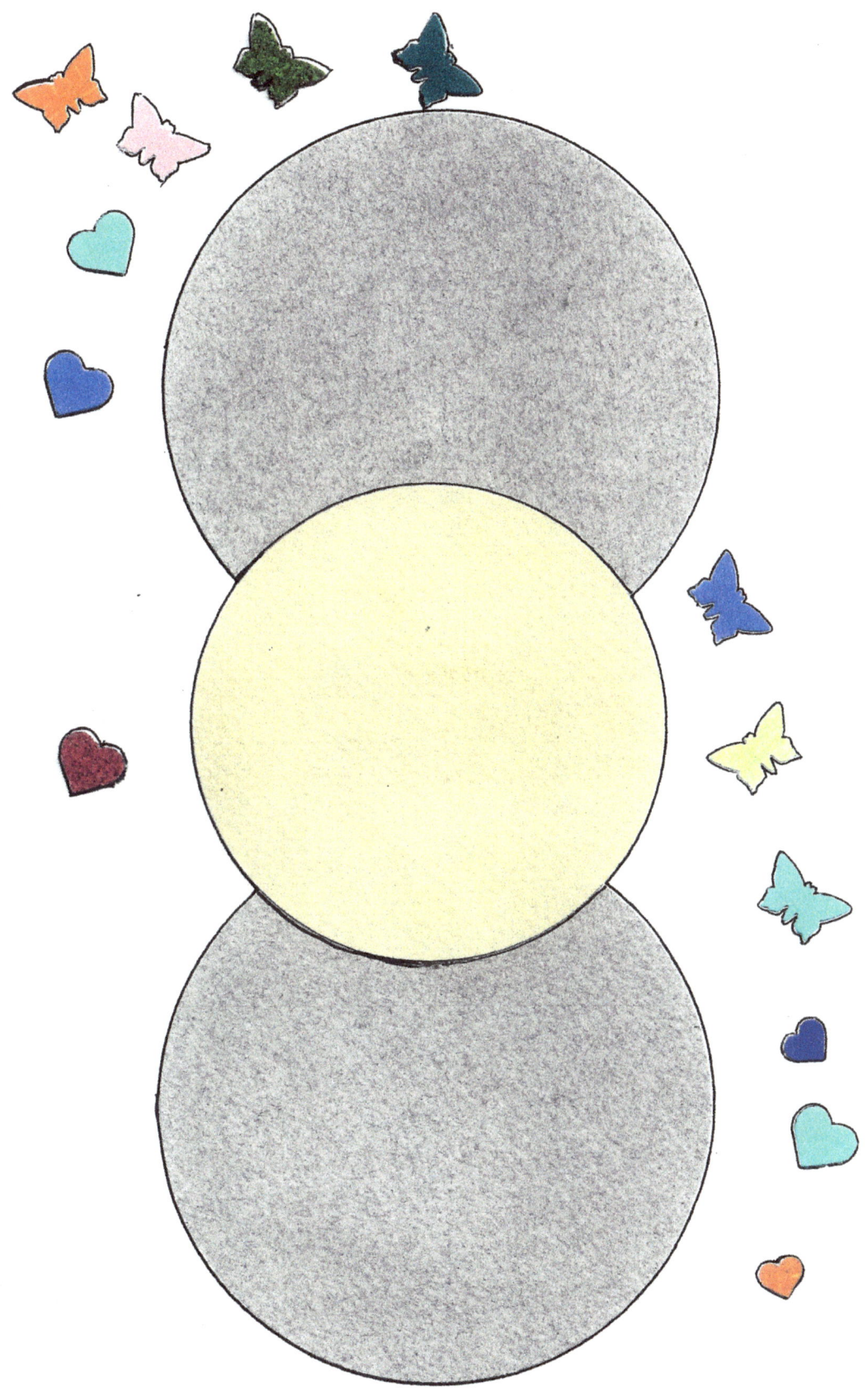

Engage in Zentangle®

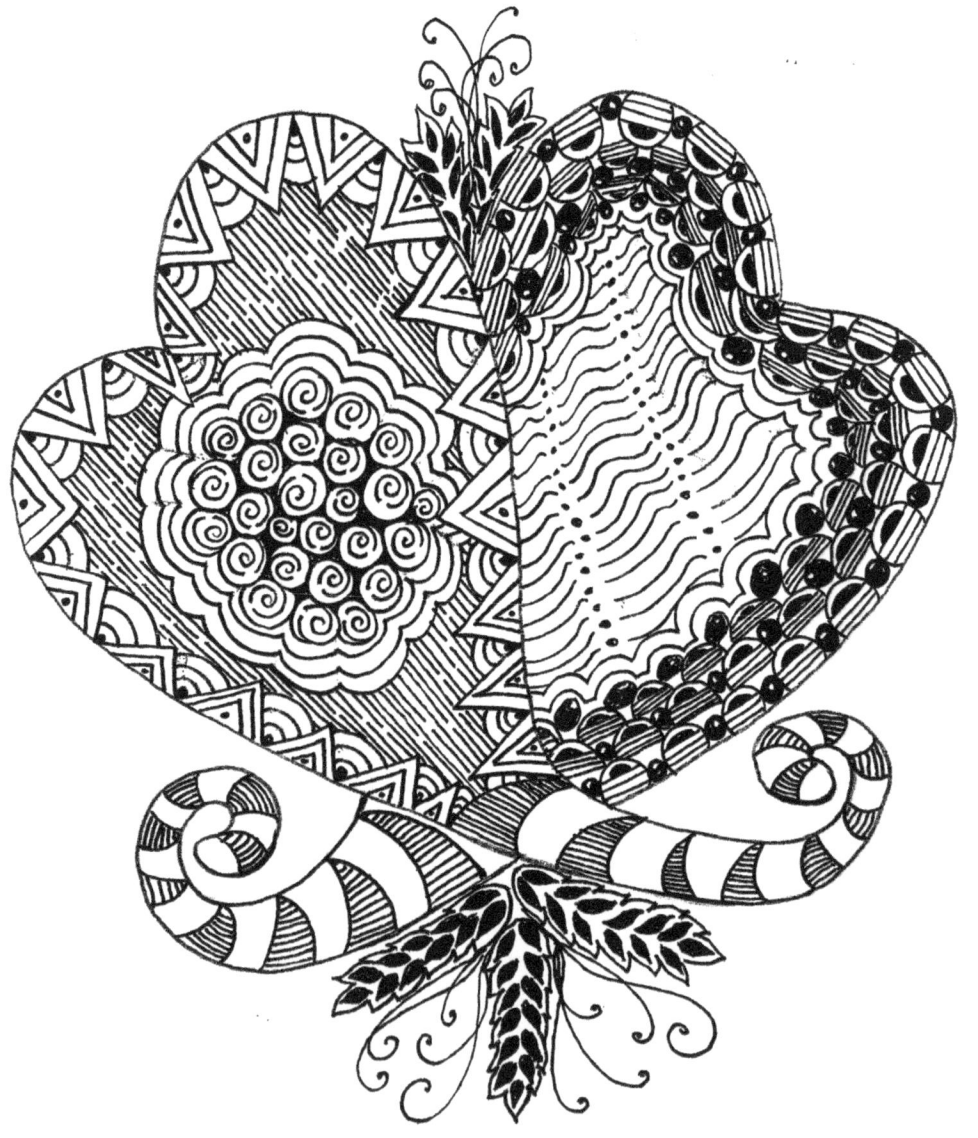

It's good for the heart...

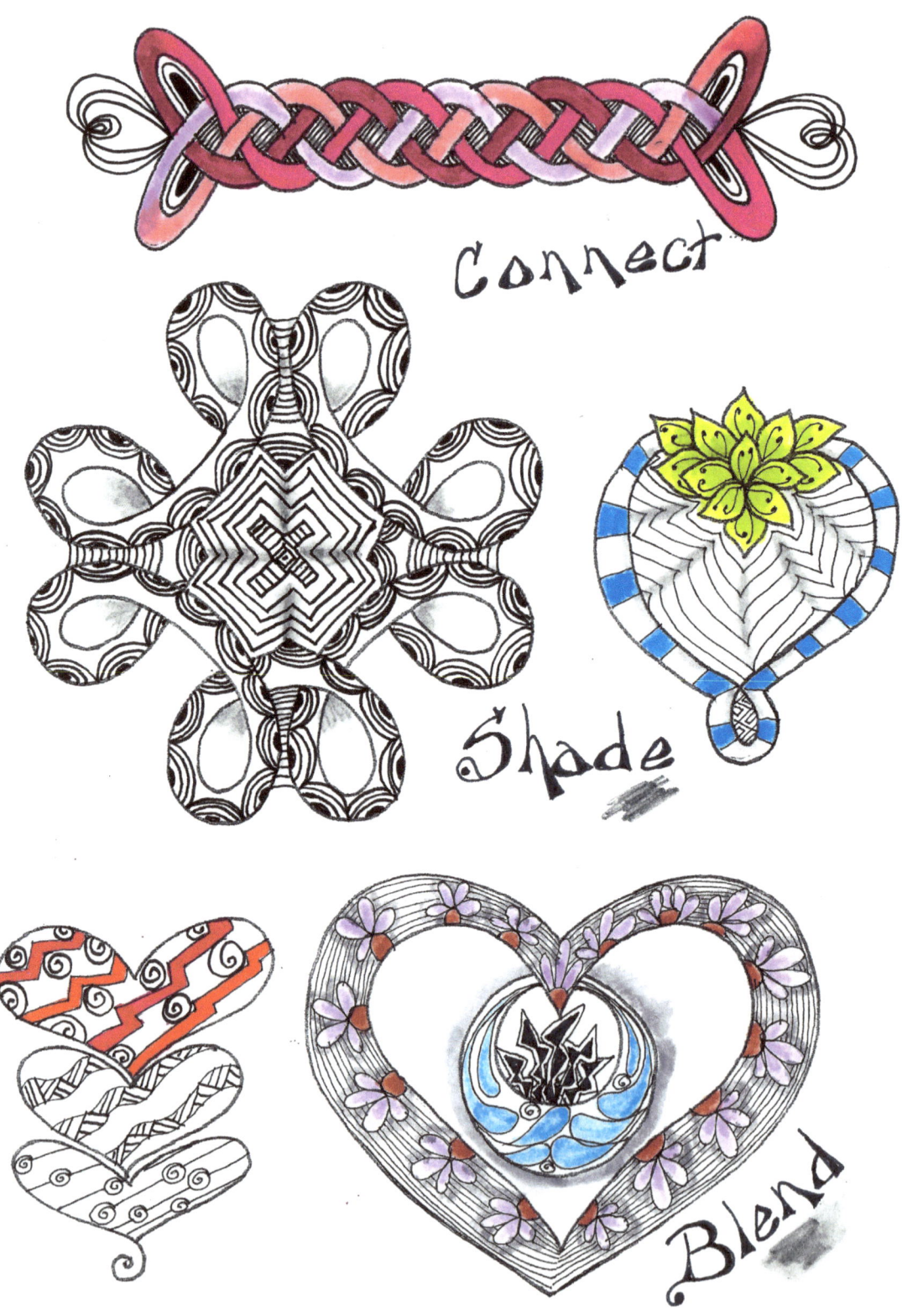

Connect

Shade

Blend

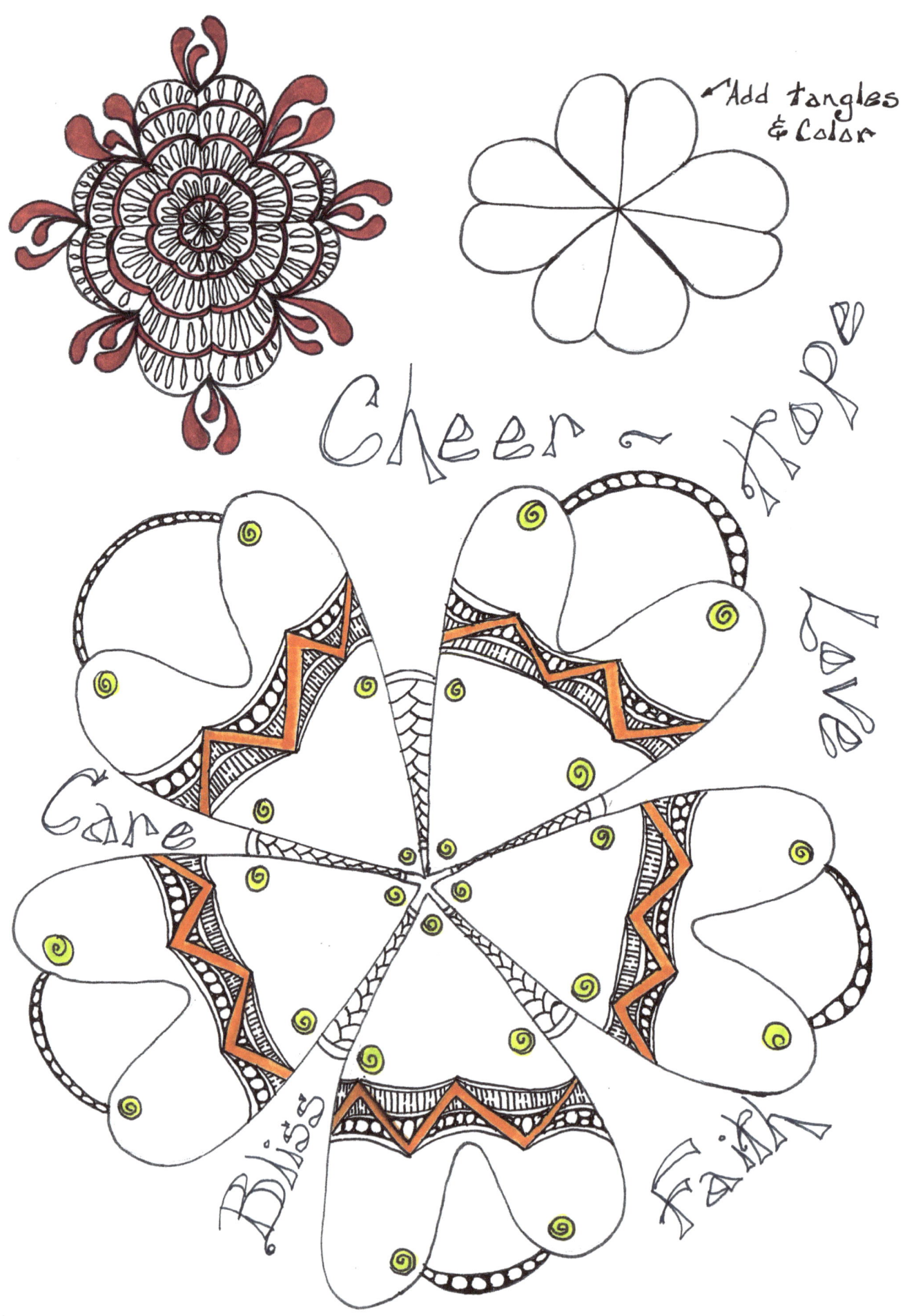

Add tangles & Color

Cheer ~ Hope

Love

Care

Faith

Bliss

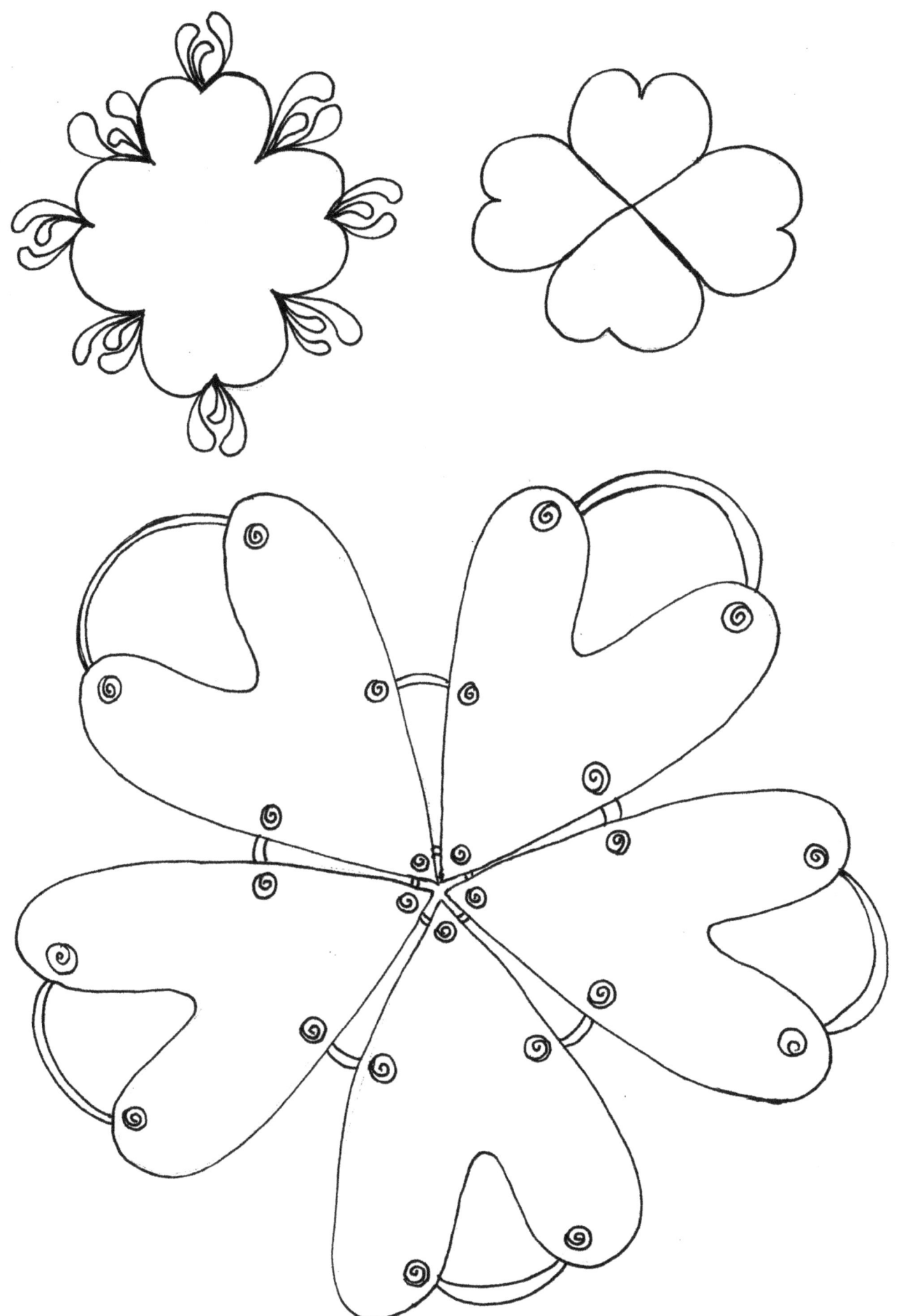

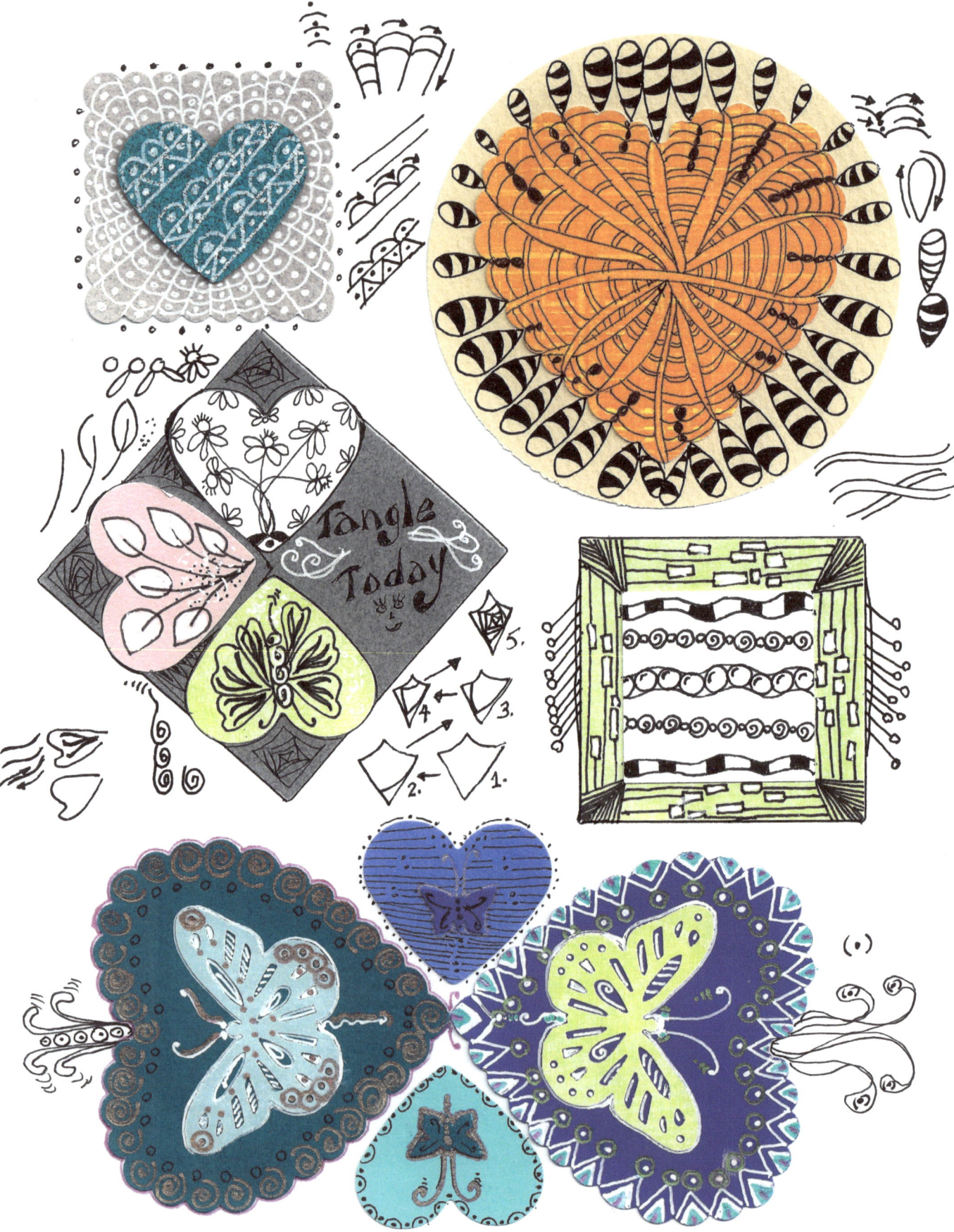

Tangle
Today

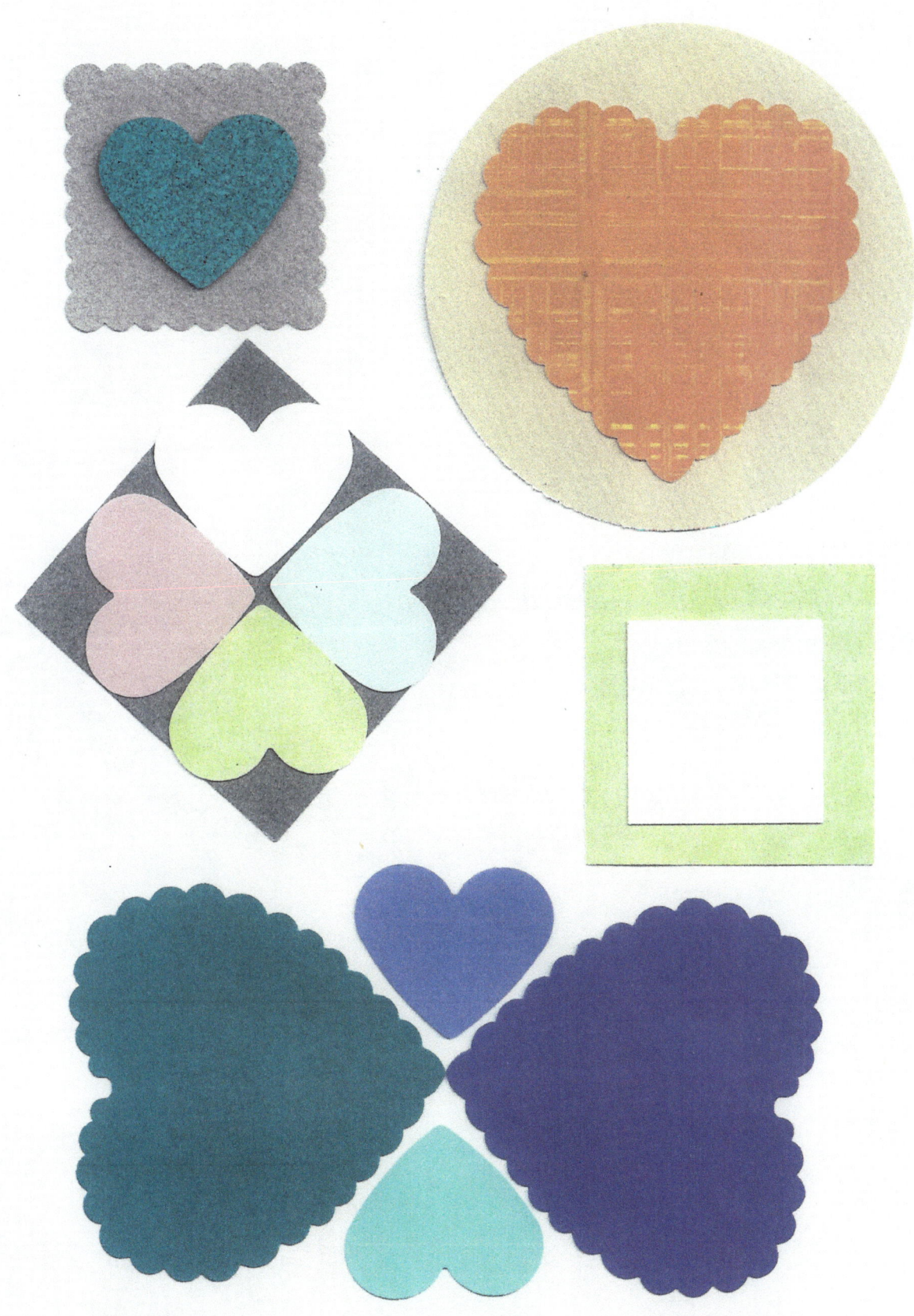

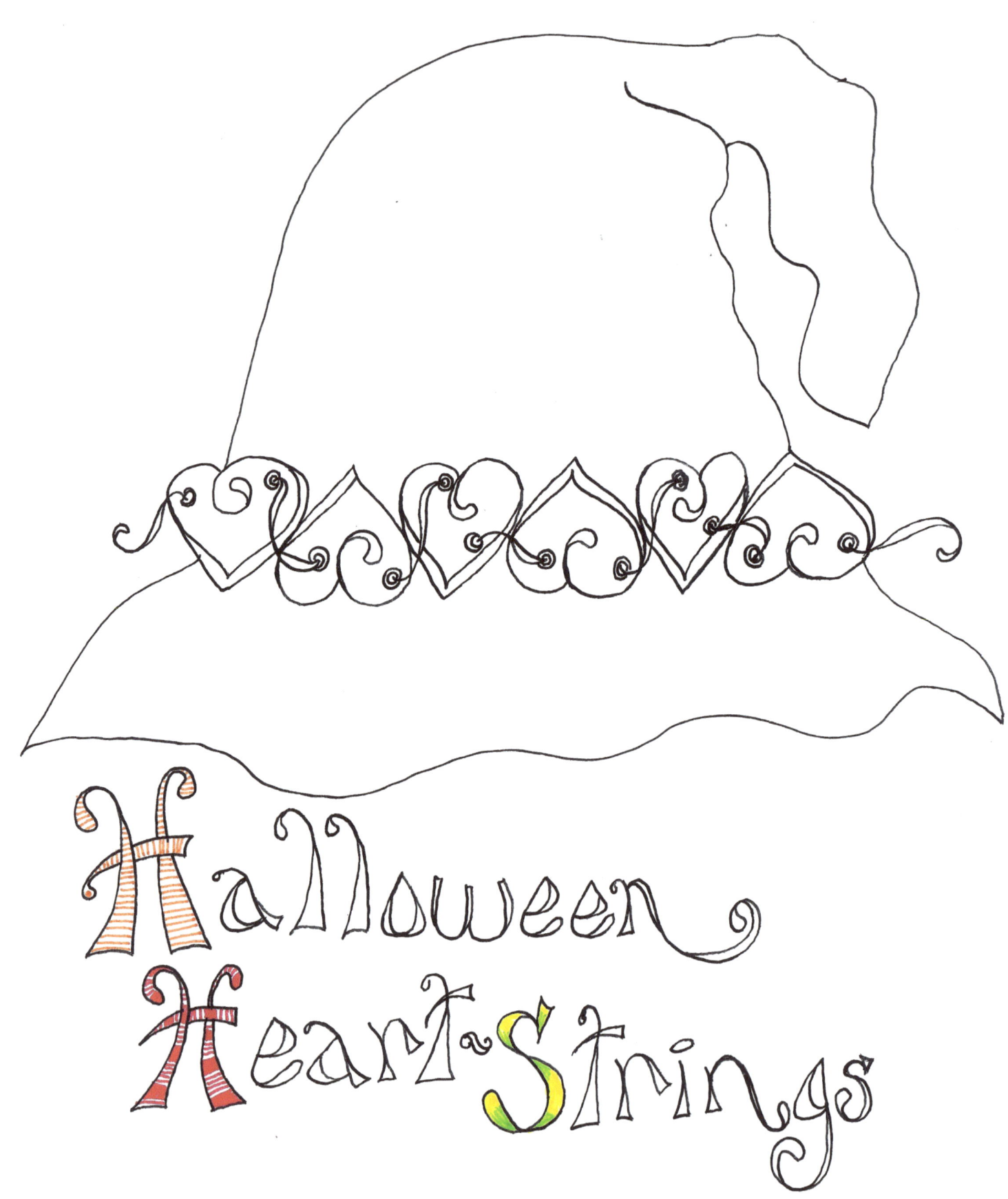

Halloween Heart-Strings

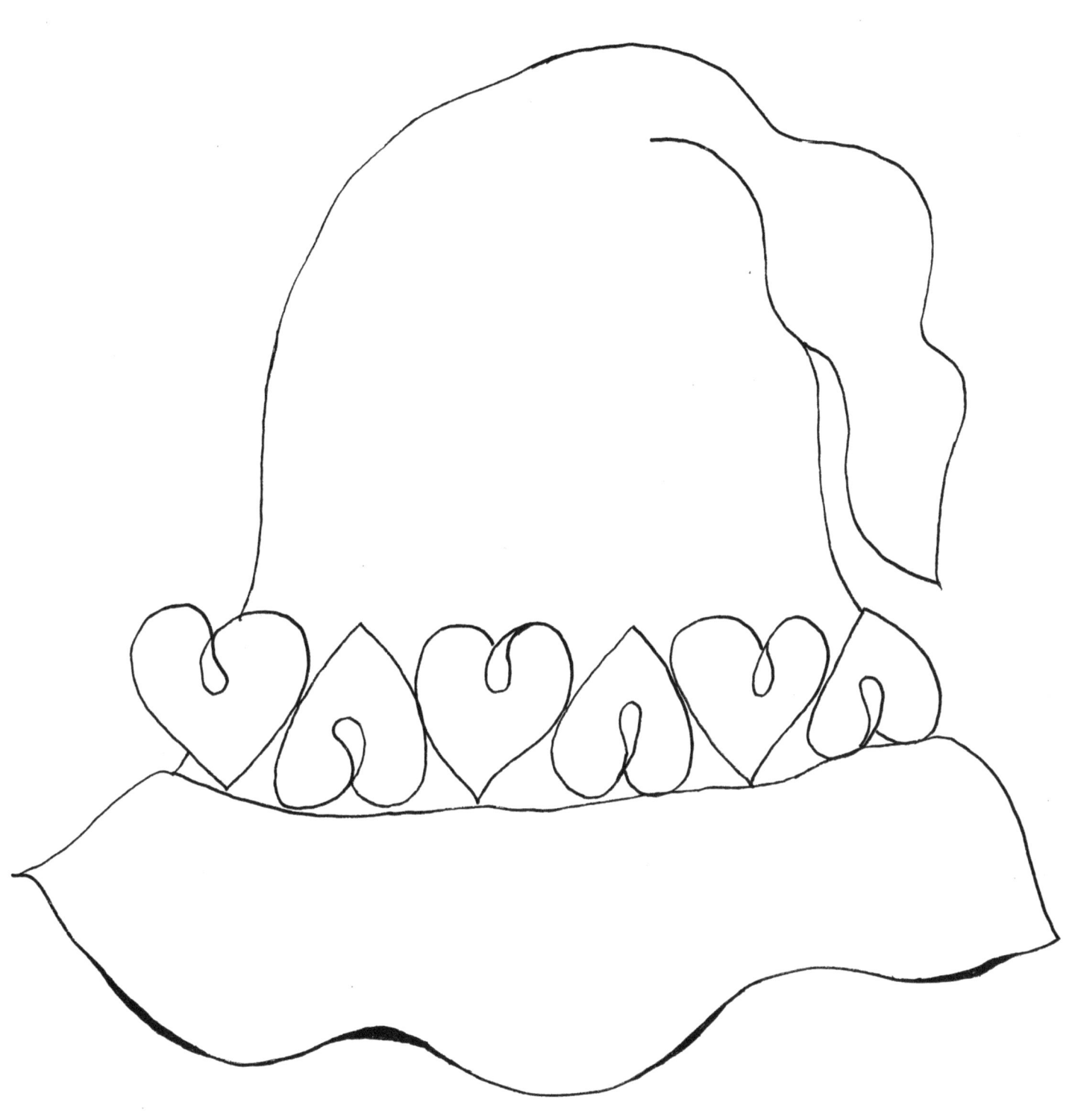

Time to Color...

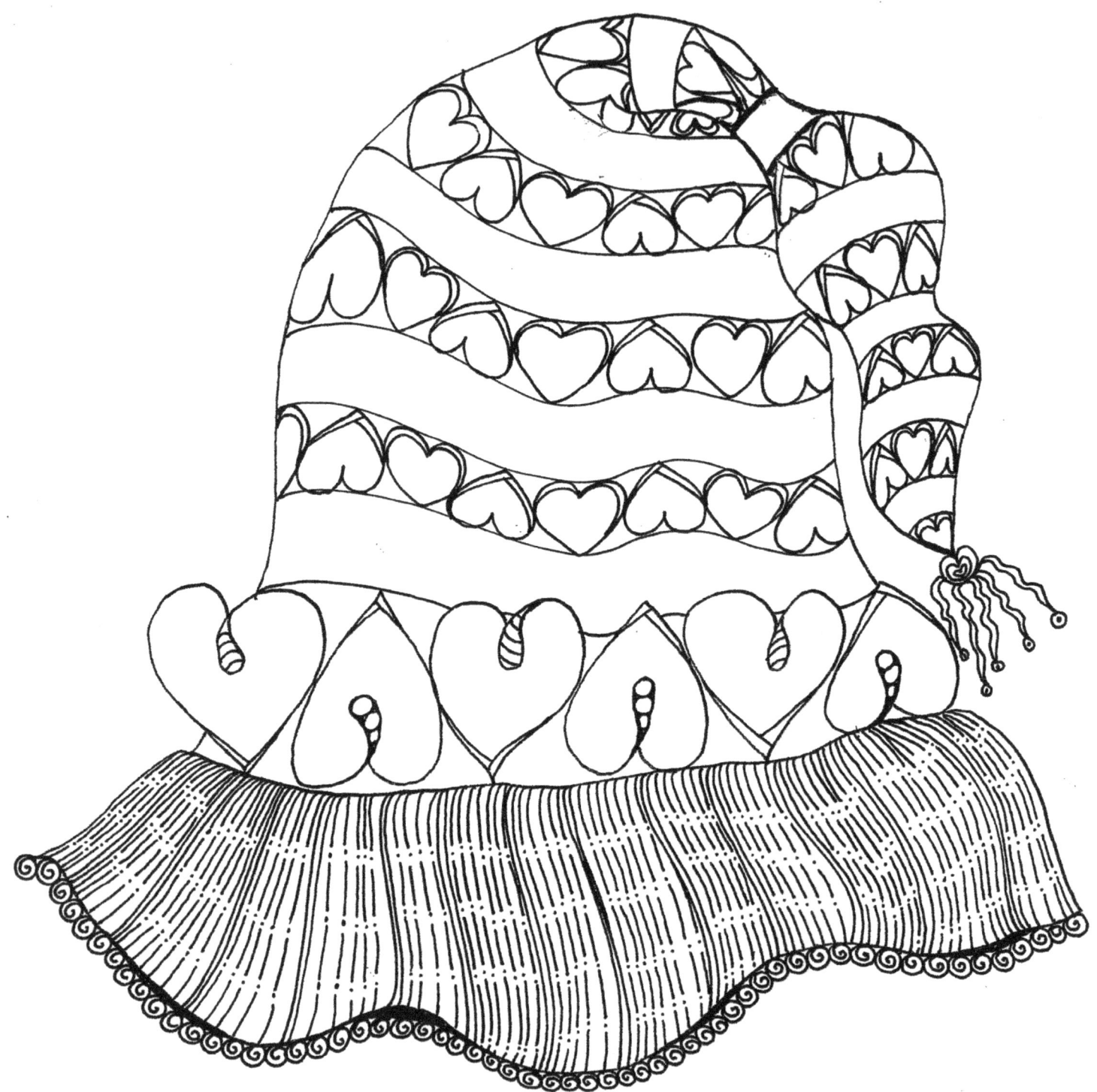

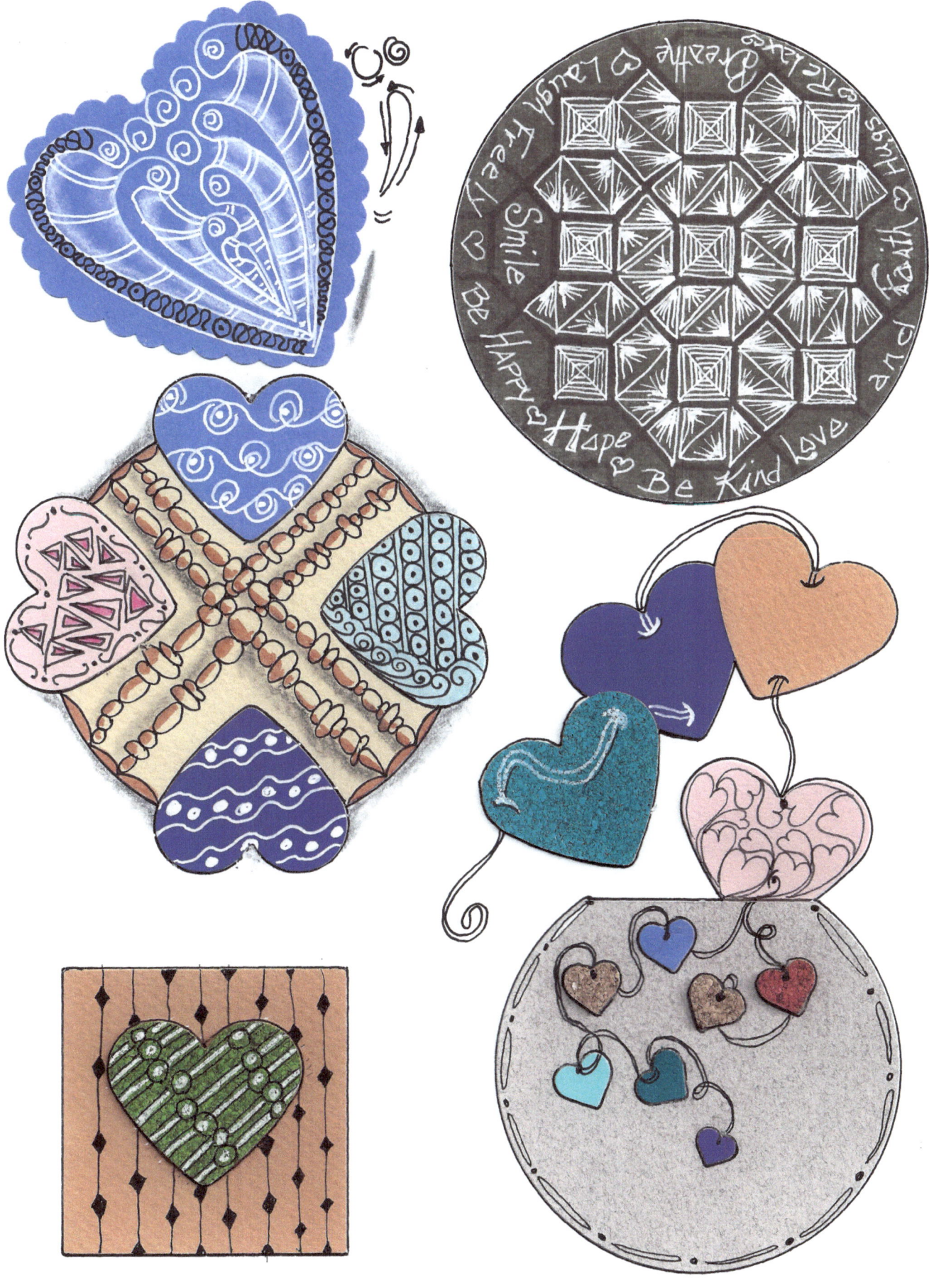

Breathe ♡ Laugh Freely ♡ Hugs ♡ Relax

Smile

Be Happy

Hope

Be Kind Love and Faith

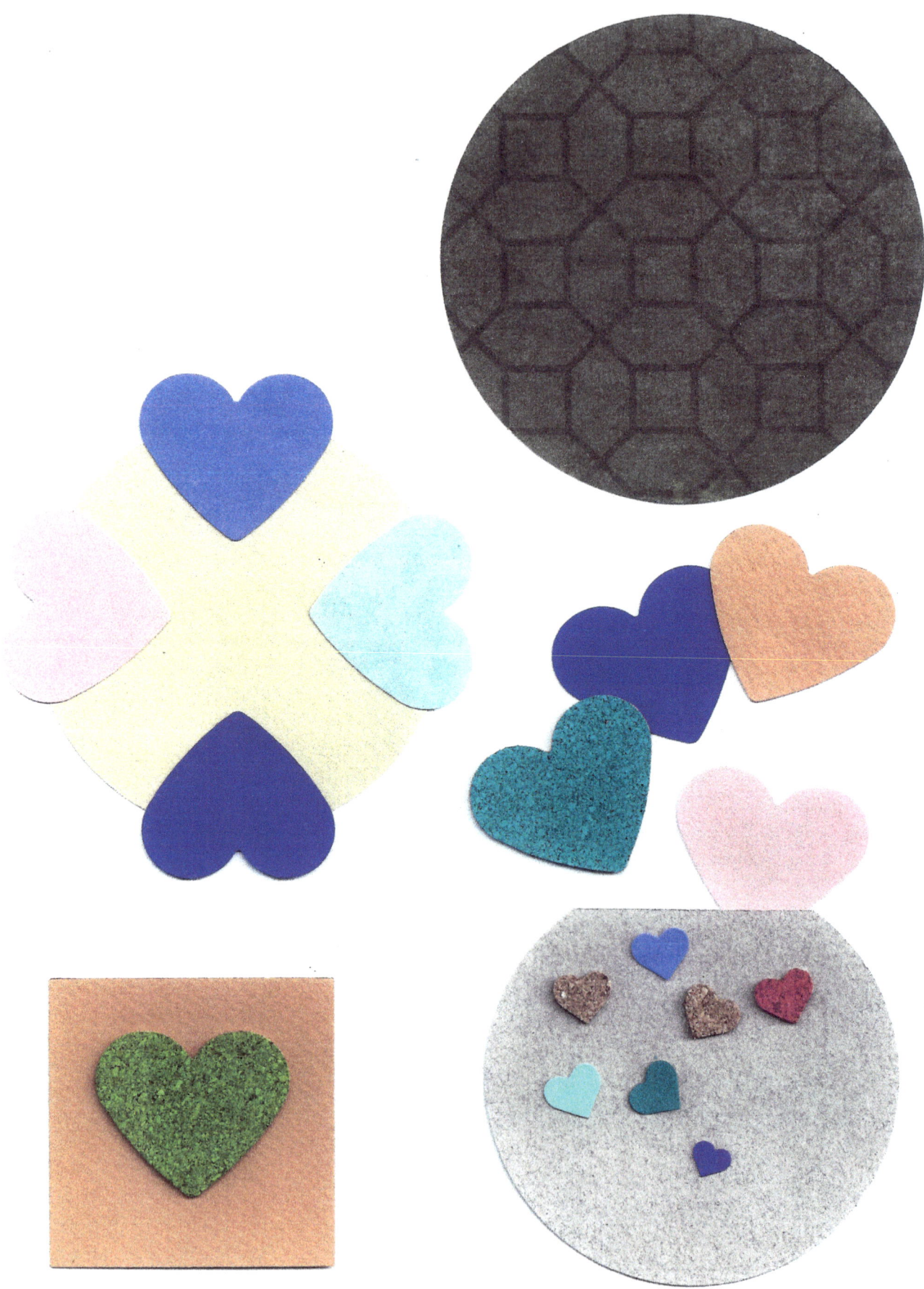

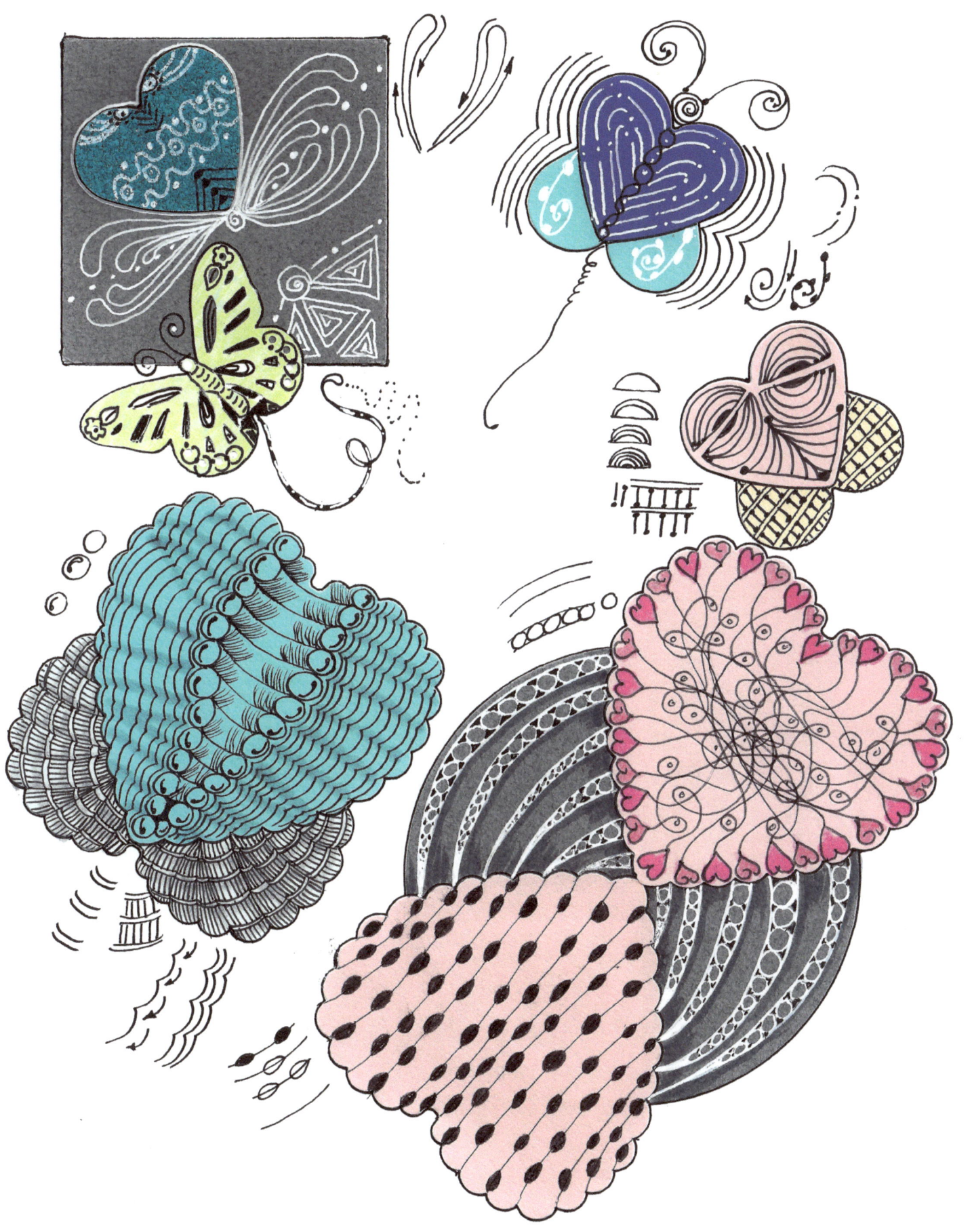

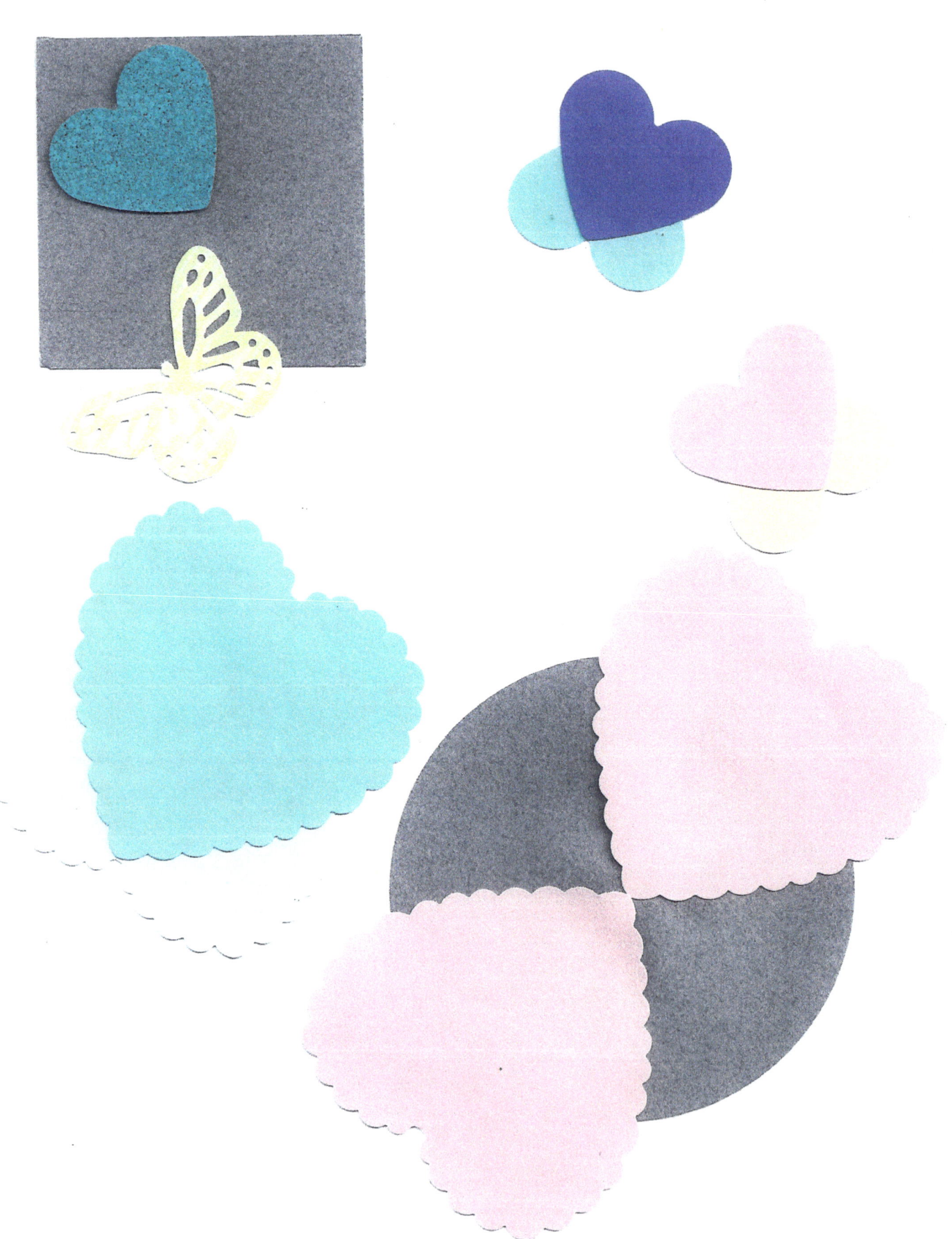

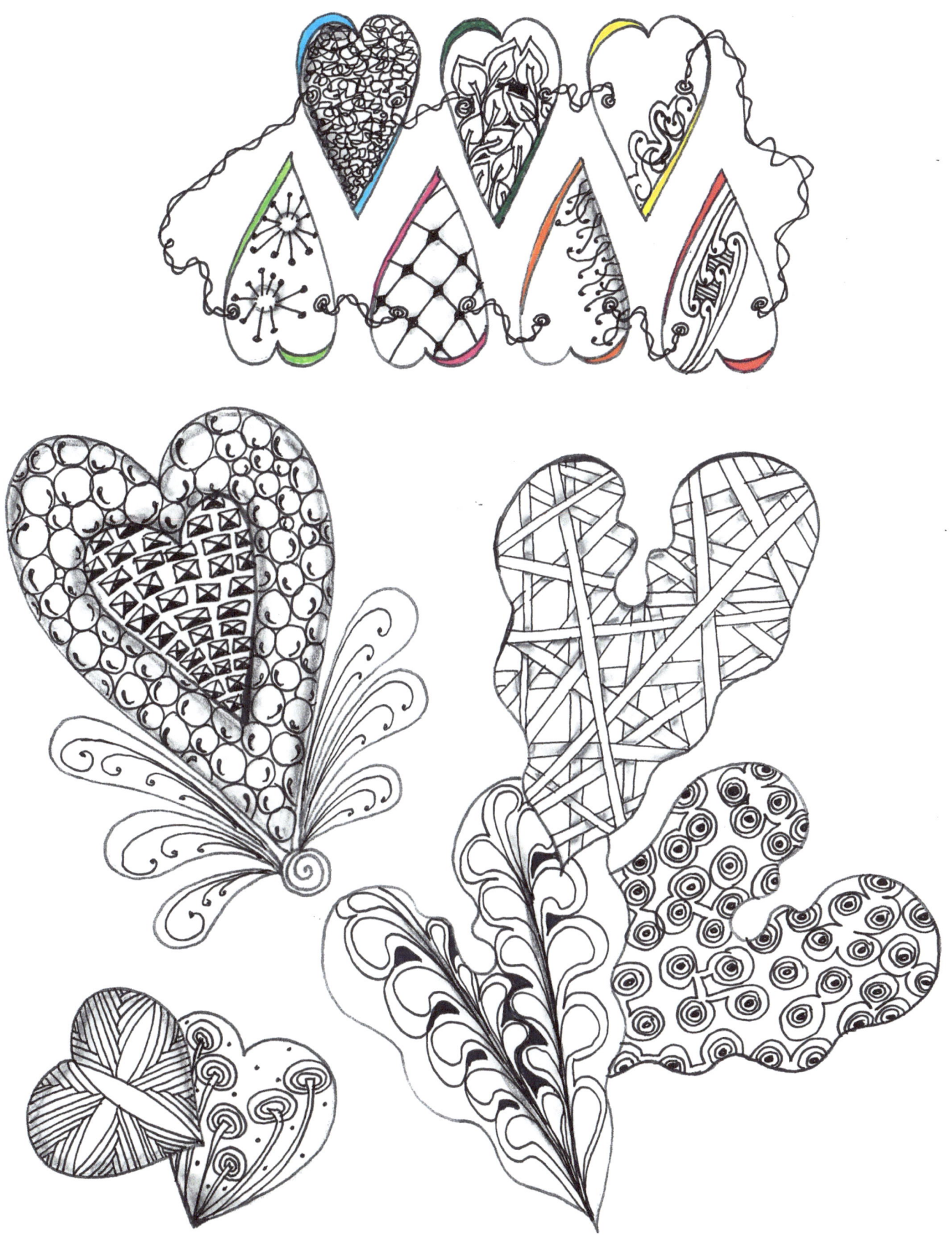

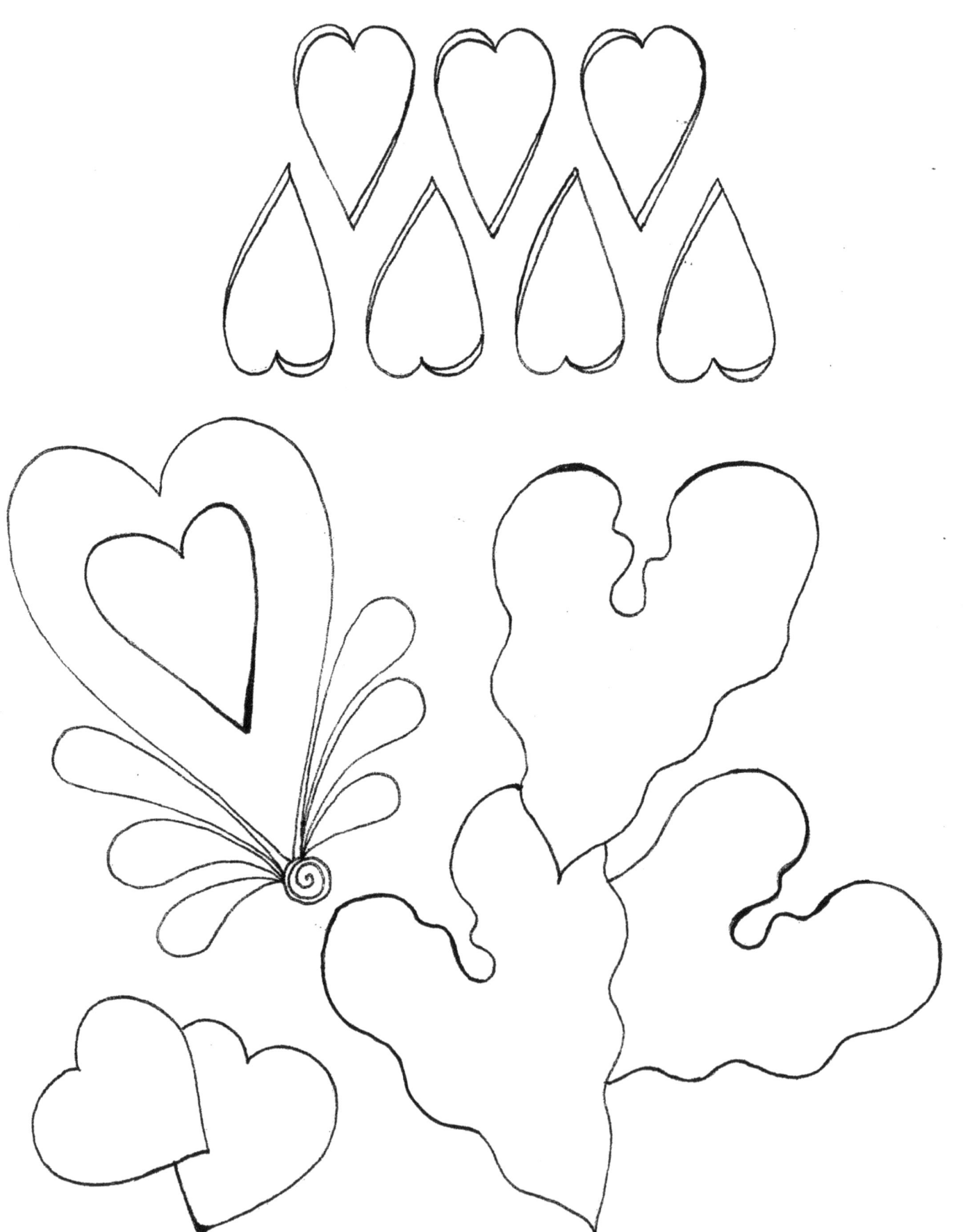

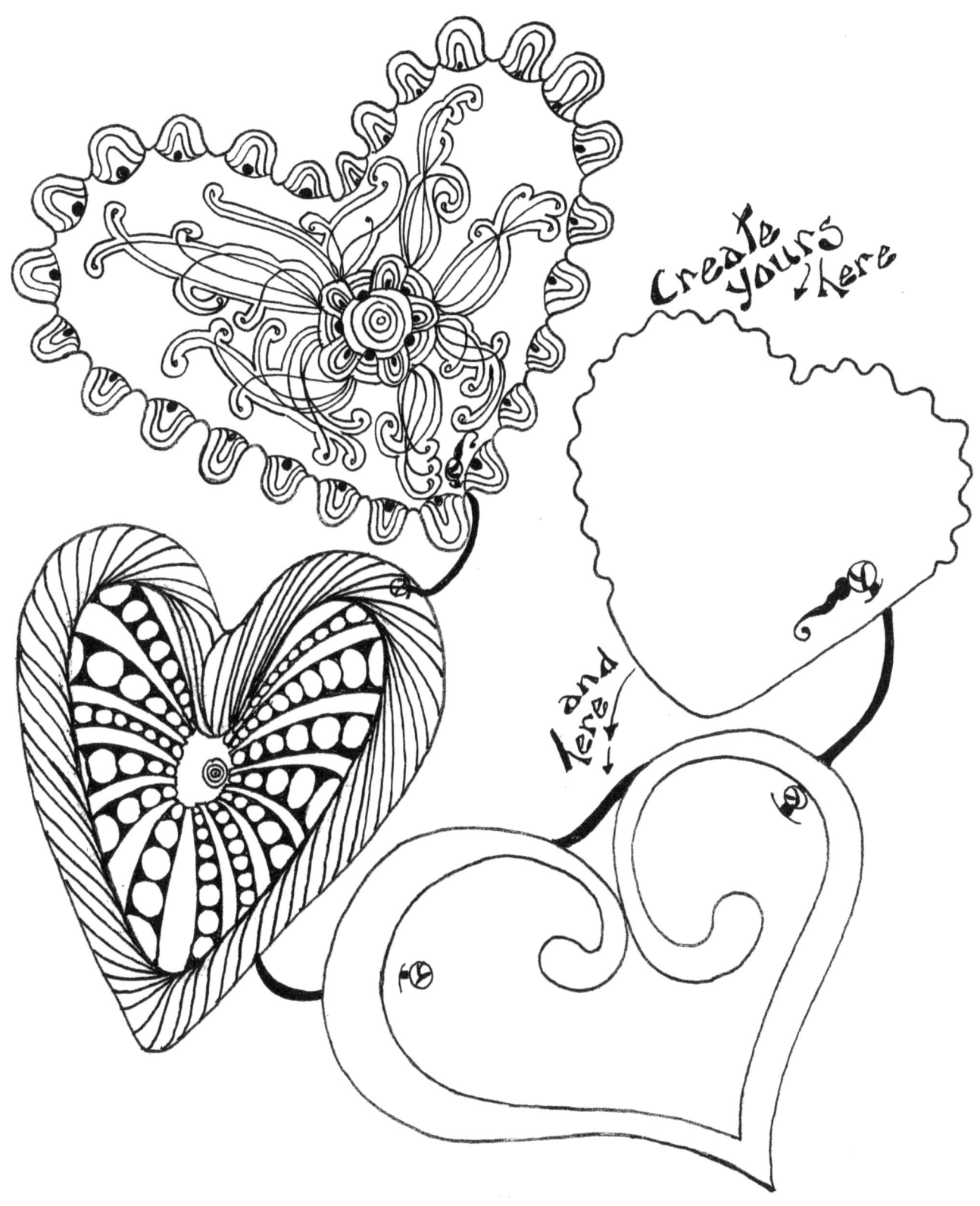

Create yours here

and here

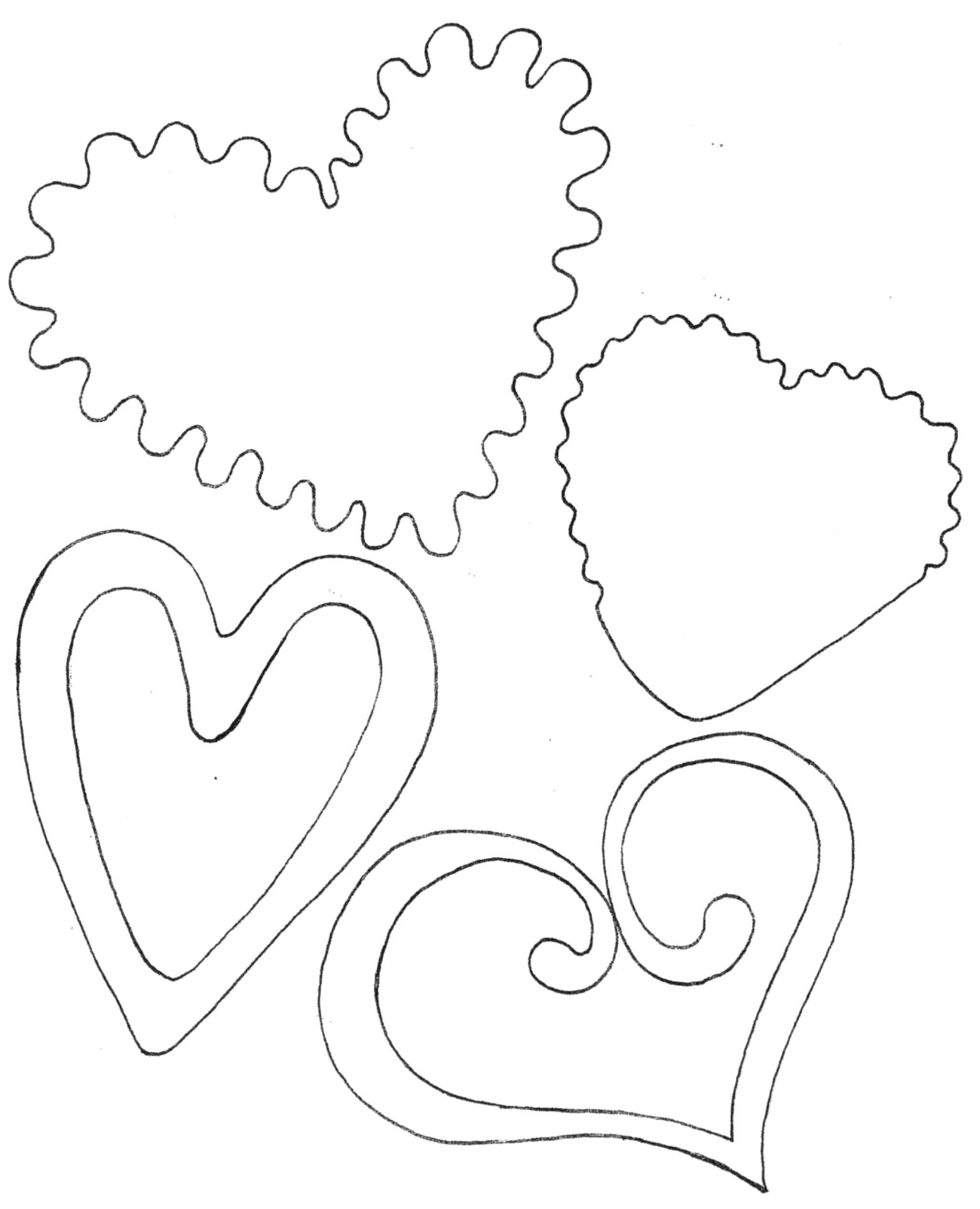

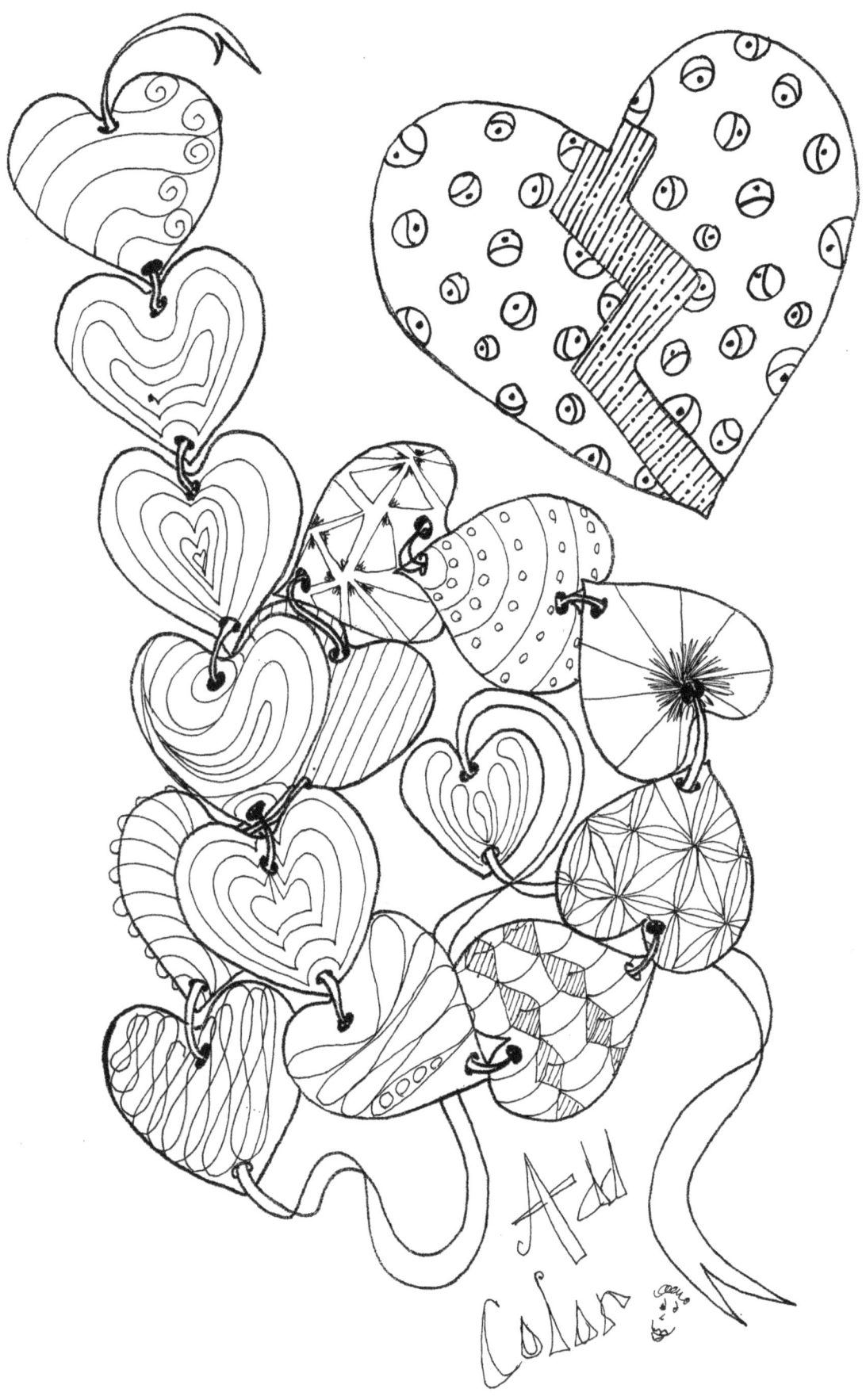

Add
Color

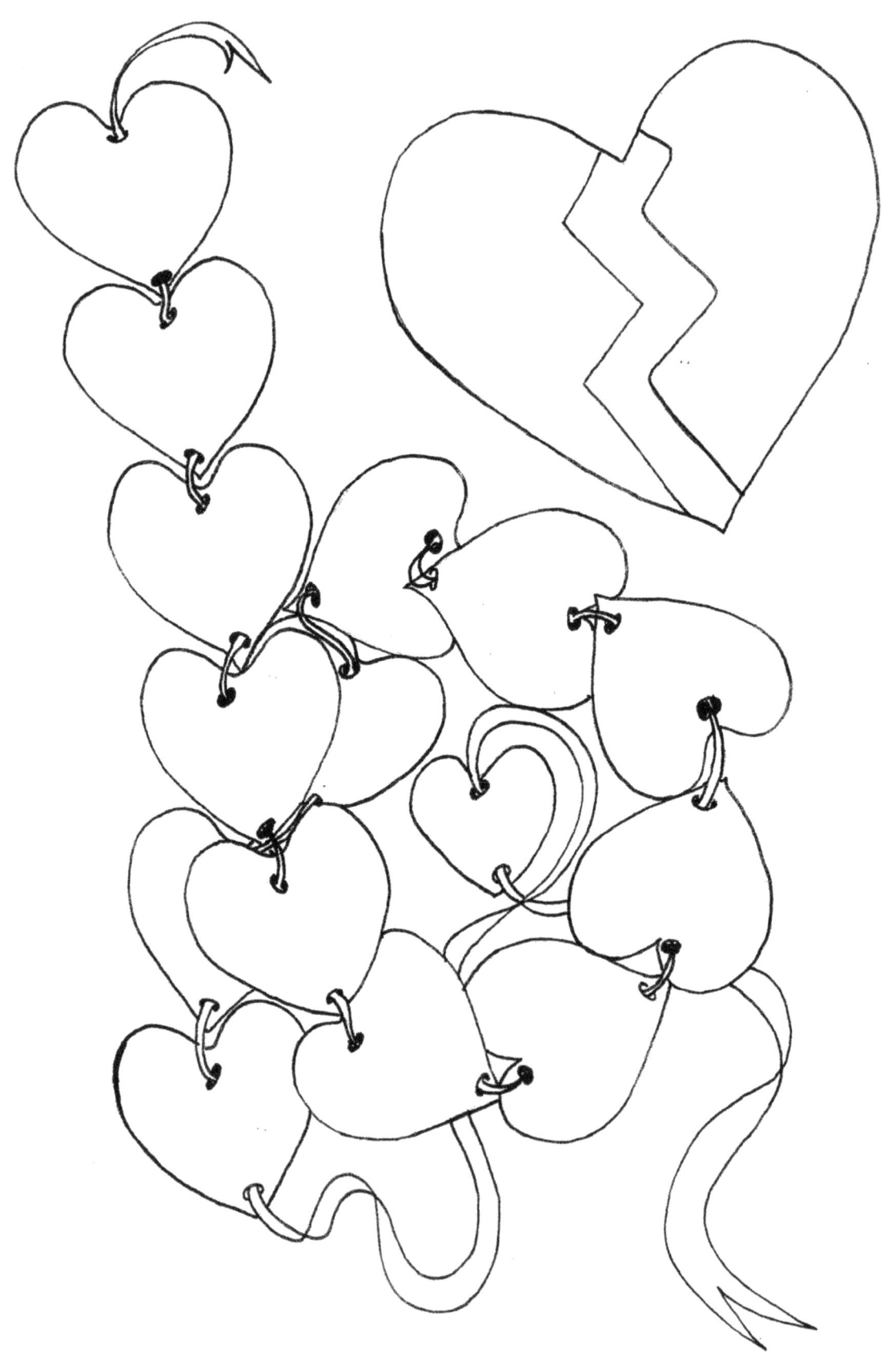

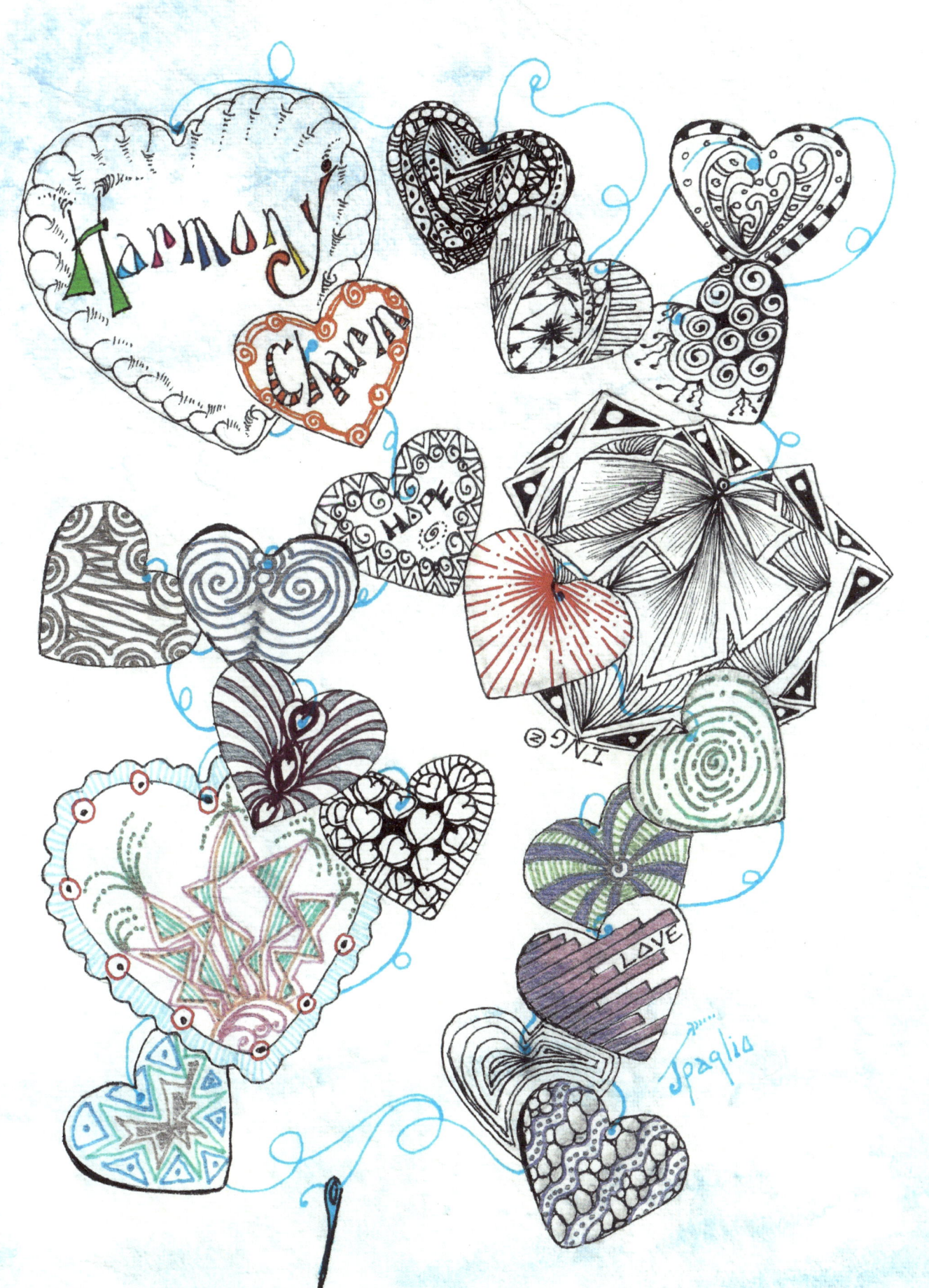

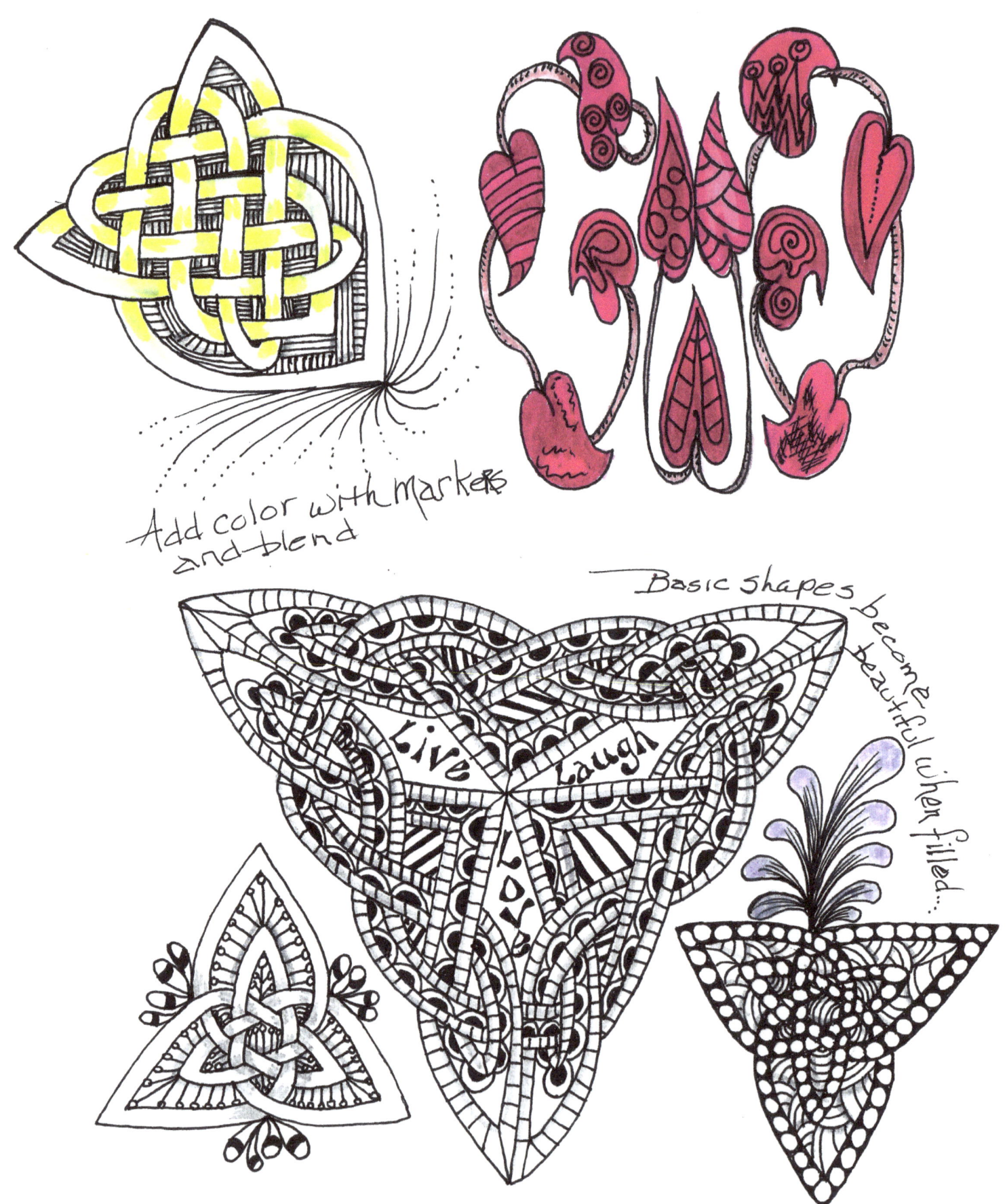

Add color with markers and blend

Basic shapes become beautiful when filled....

Live Laugh [Love]

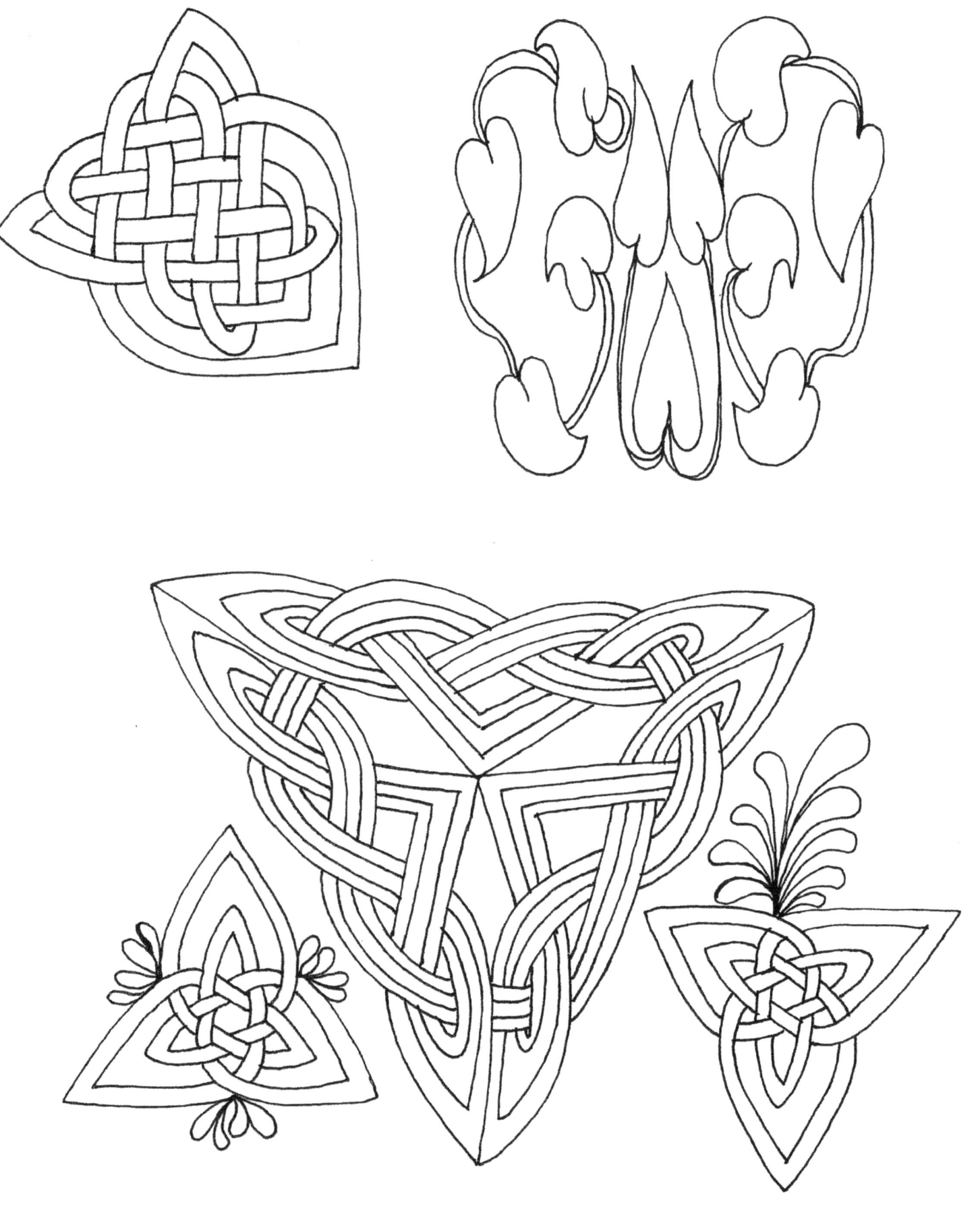

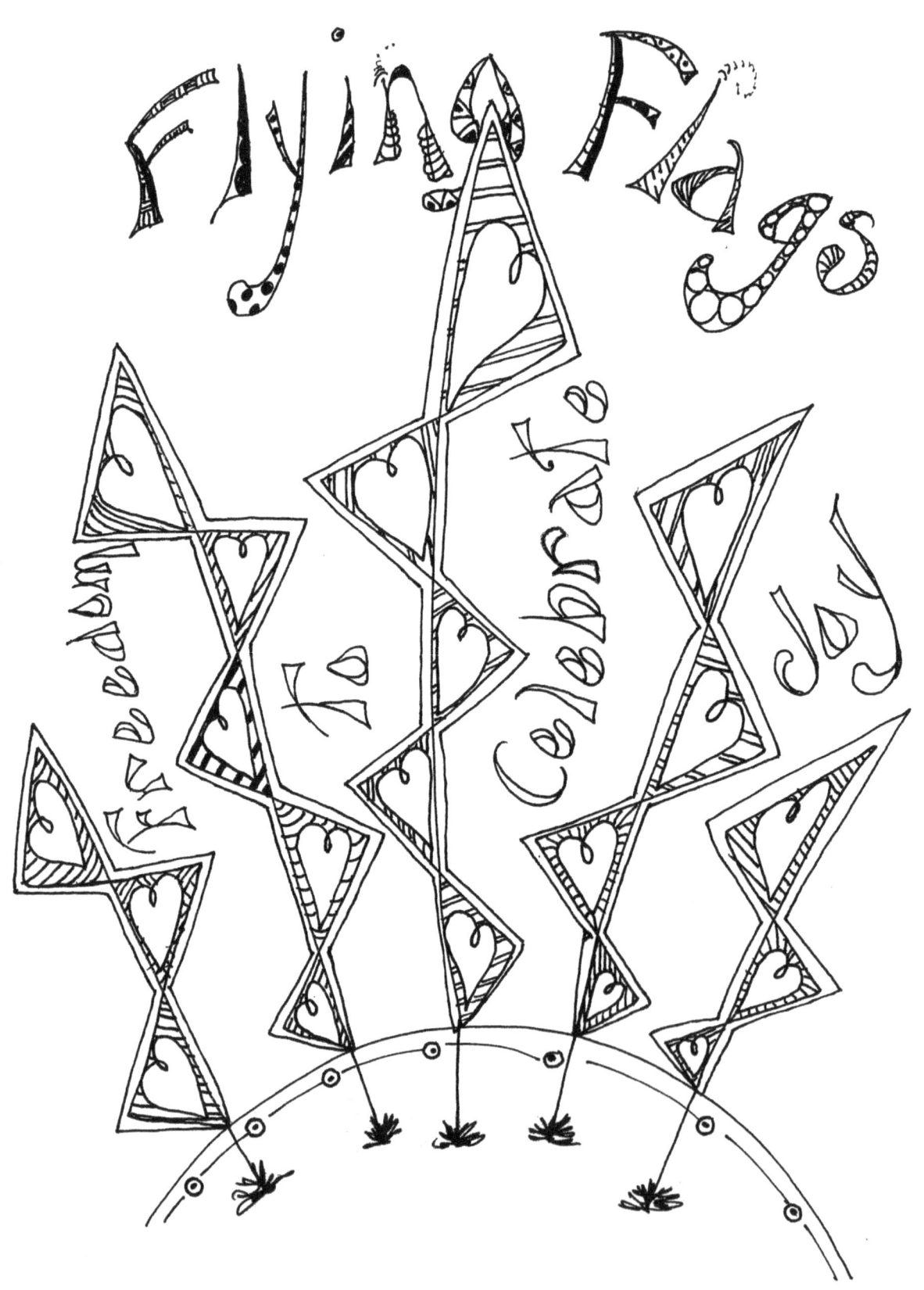

Tangle Your Flags

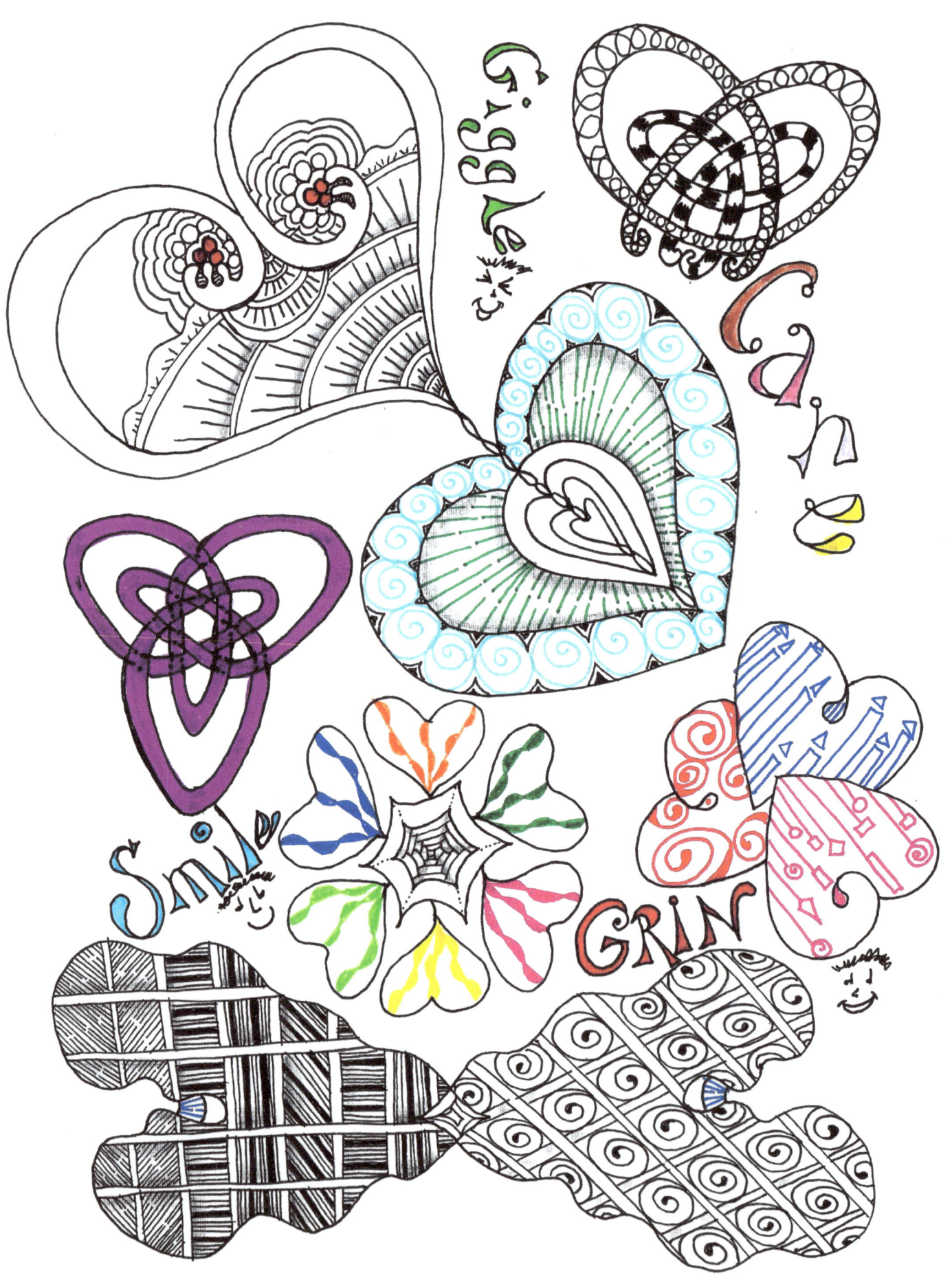

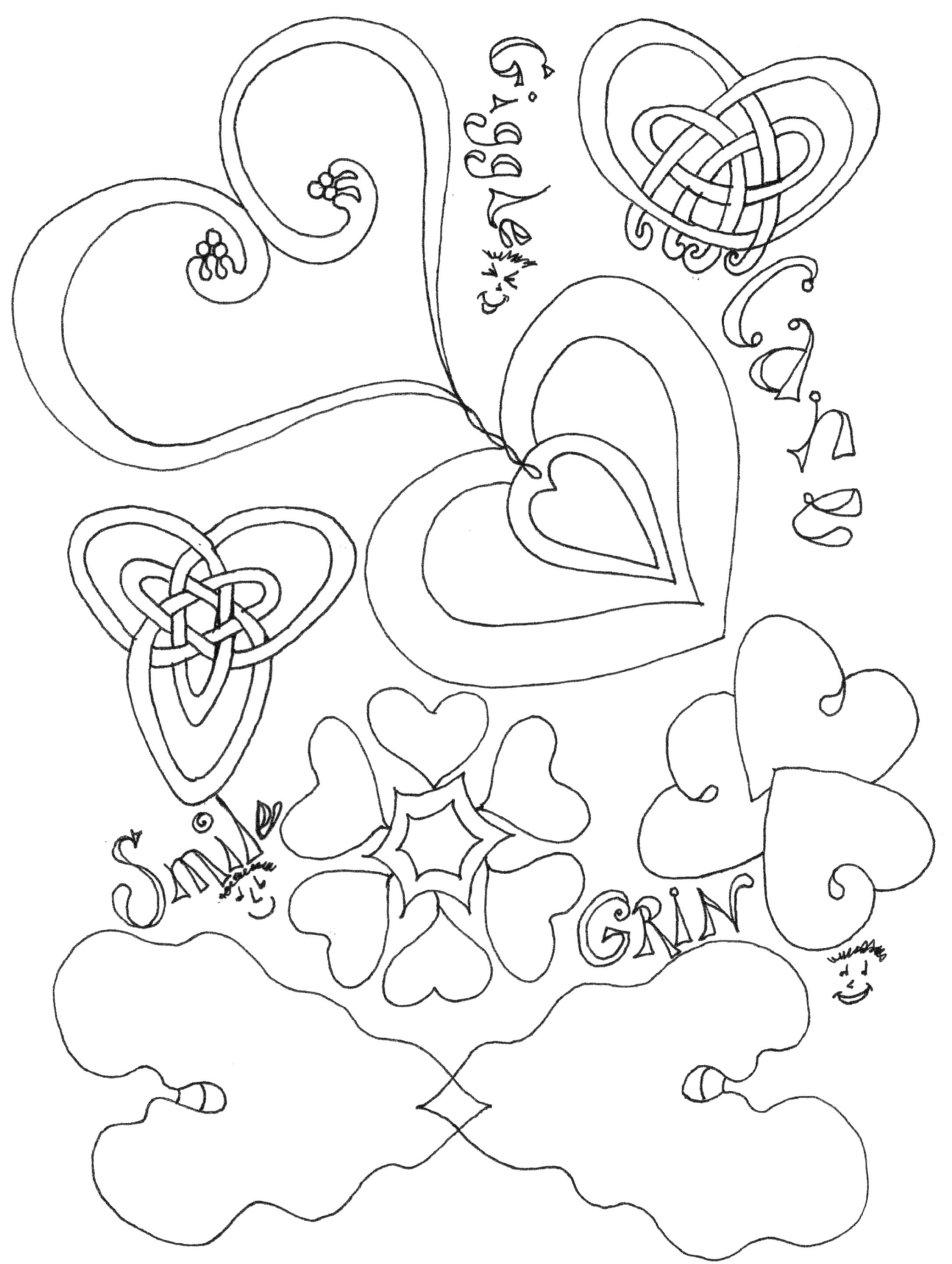

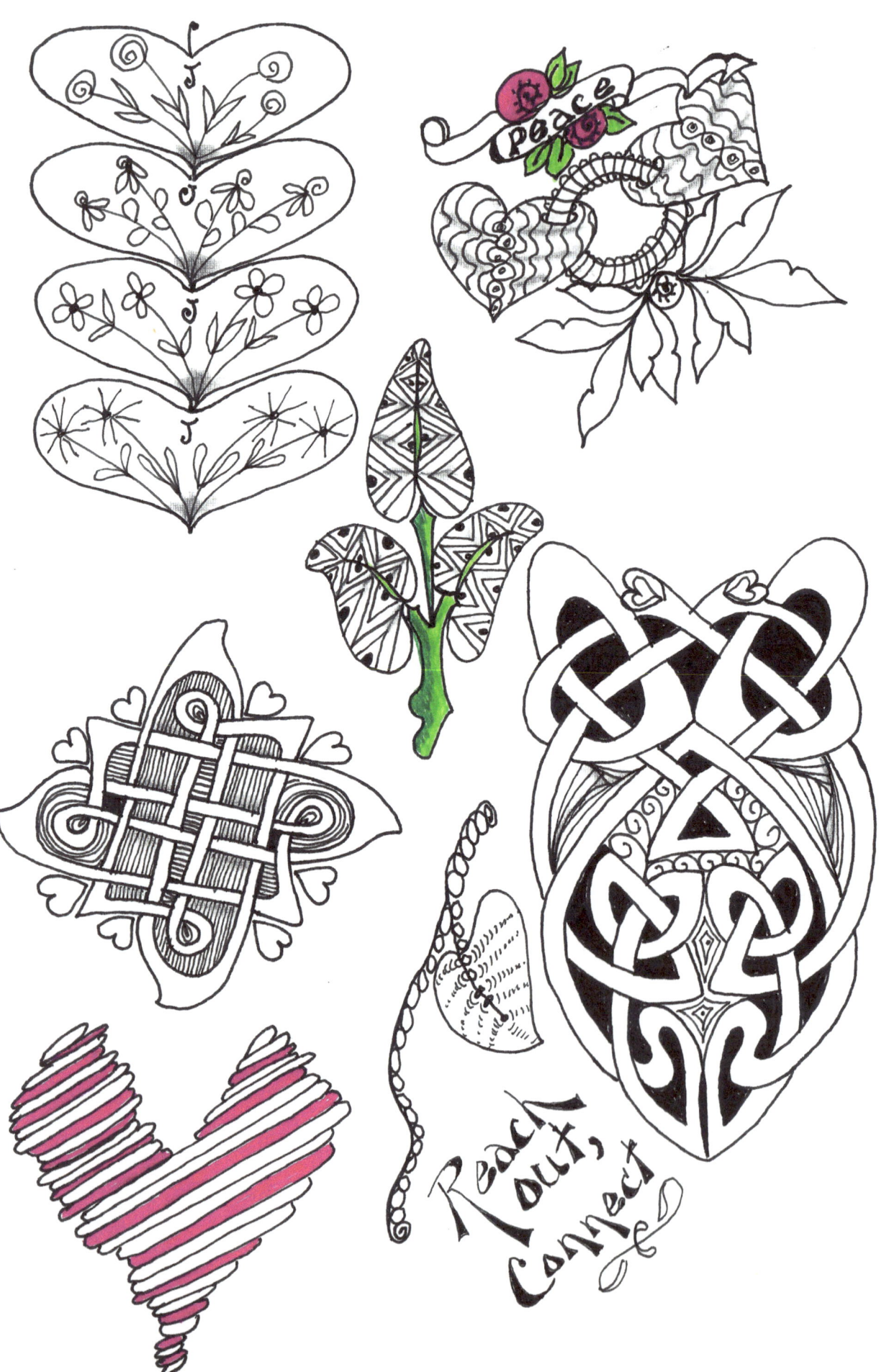

Peace

Reach out, Connect

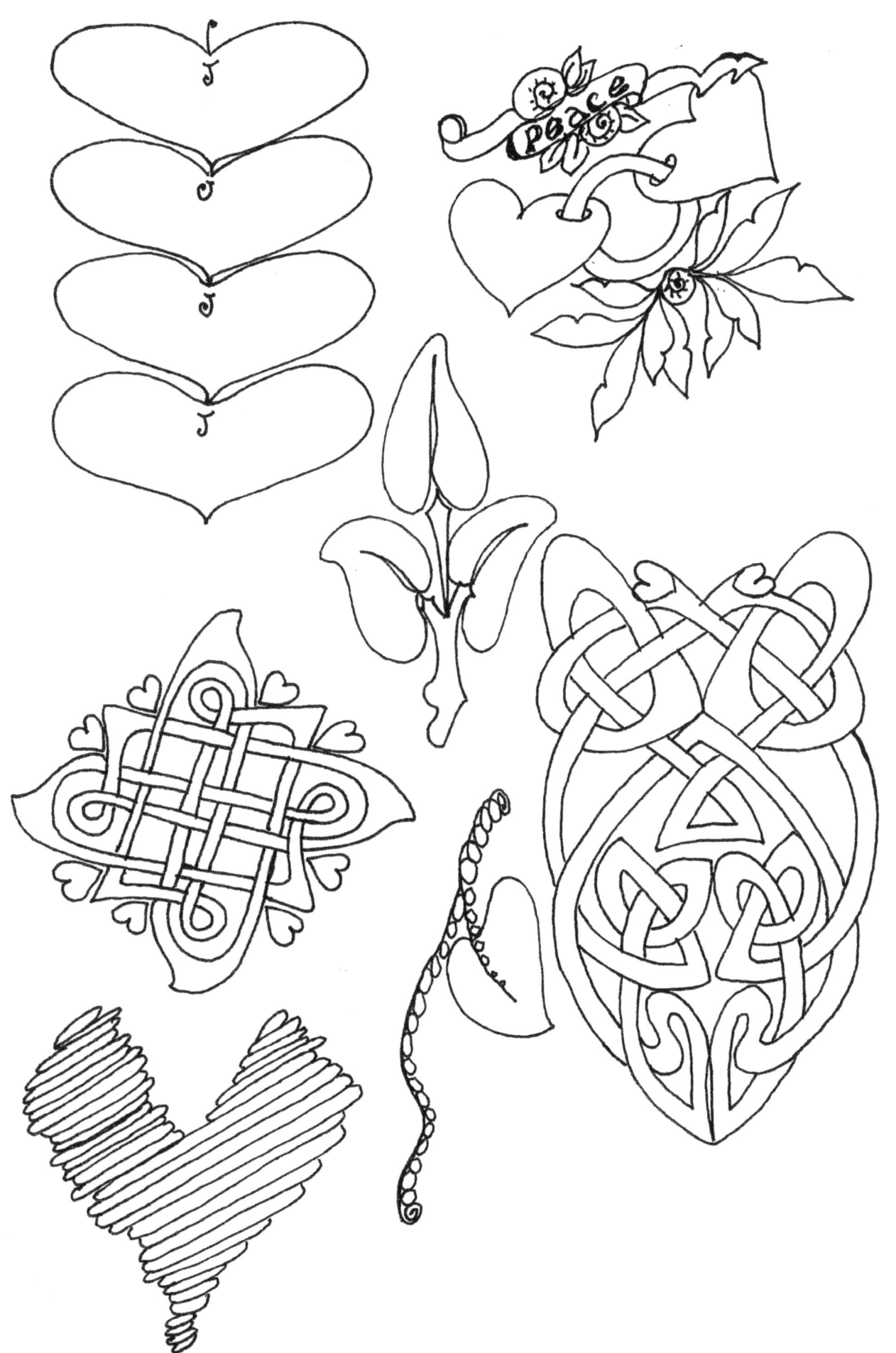

peace

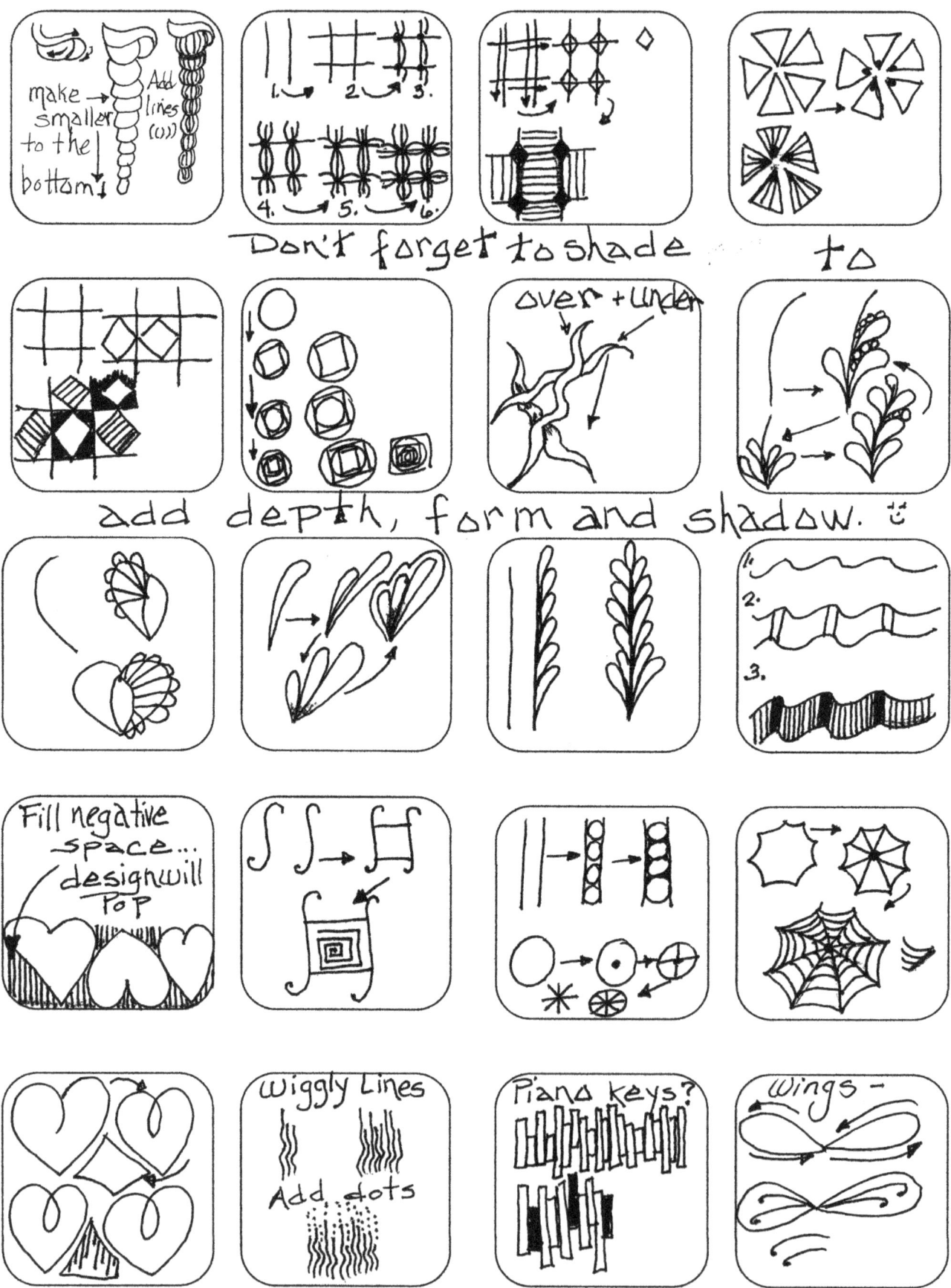

Don't forget to shade to add depth, form and shadow.

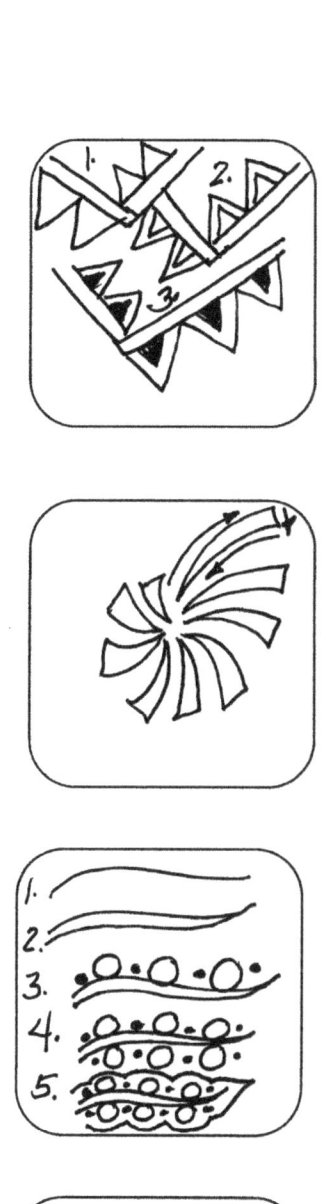

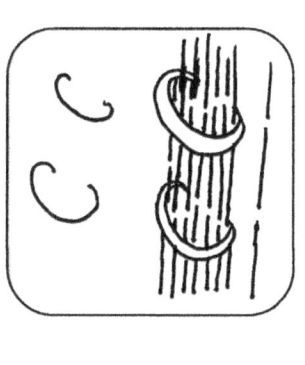

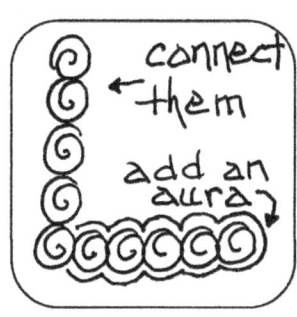

connect them

add an aura

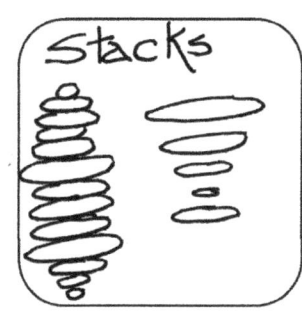

stacks

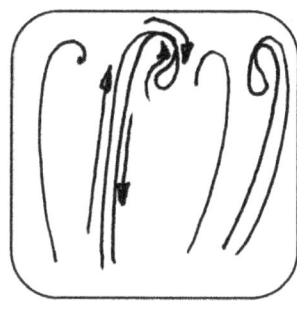

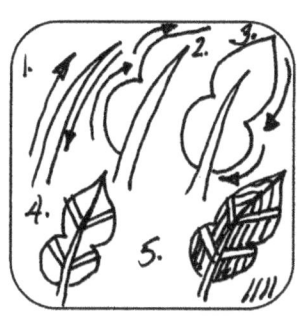

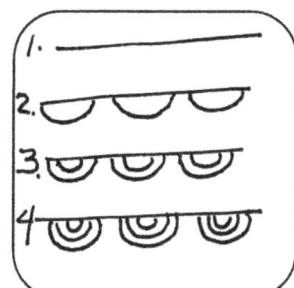

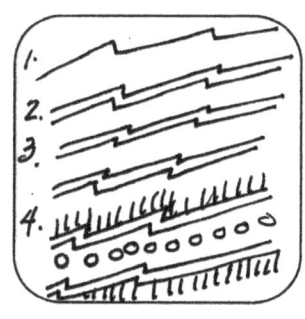

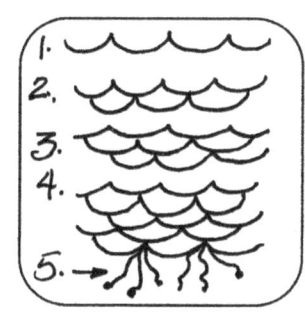

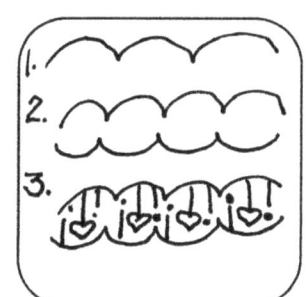

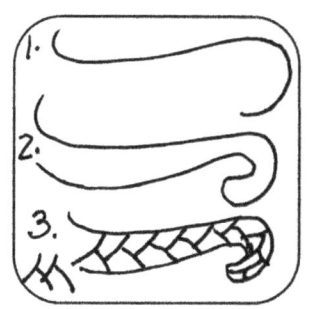

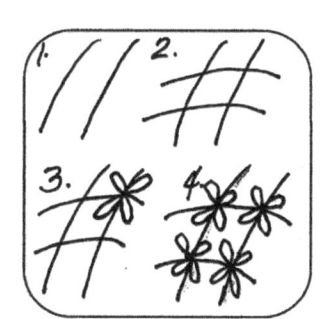

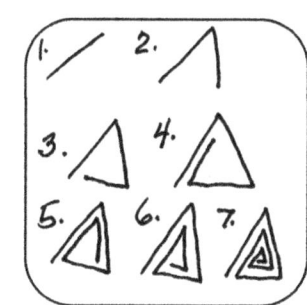

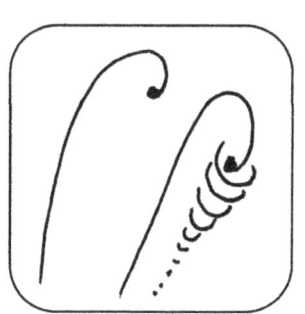

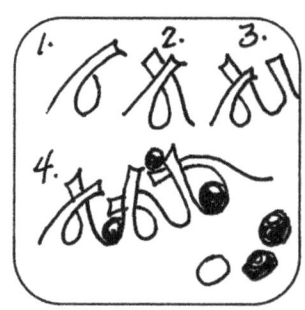

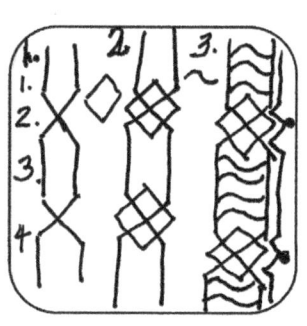

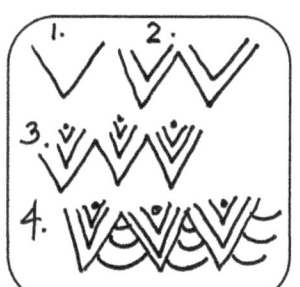

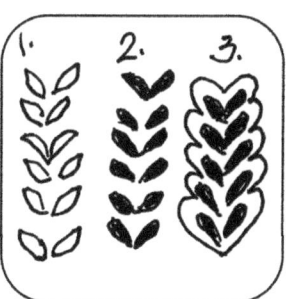

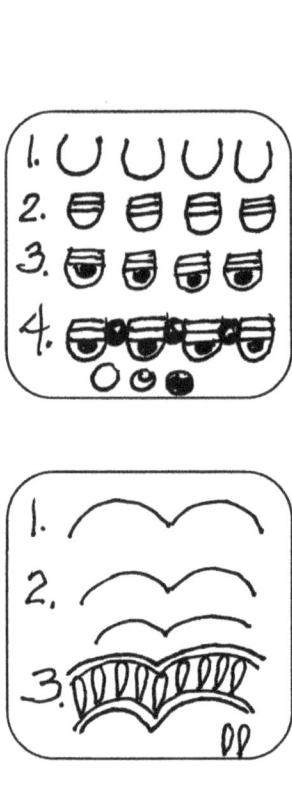 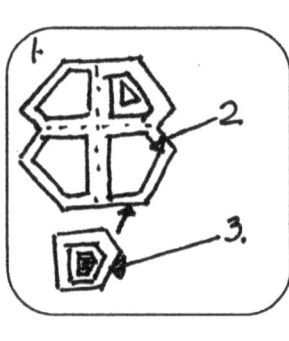 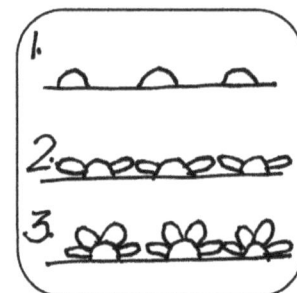 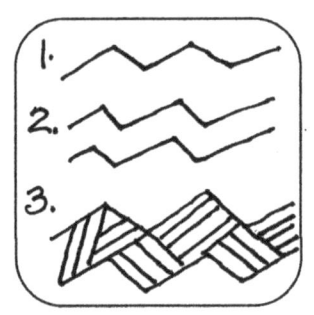

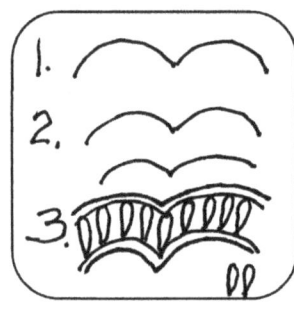 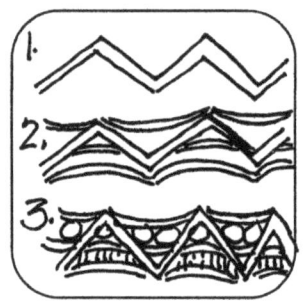 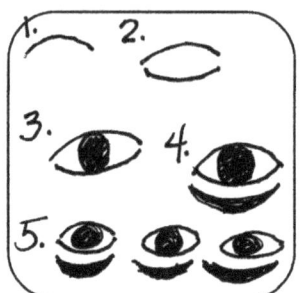 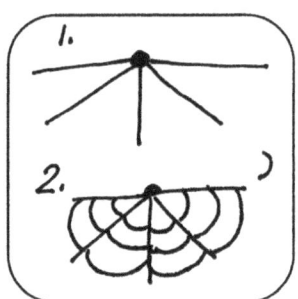

  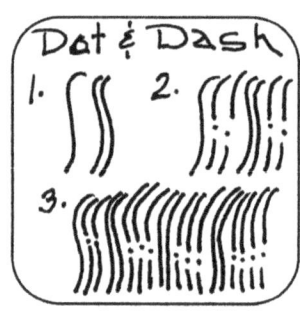 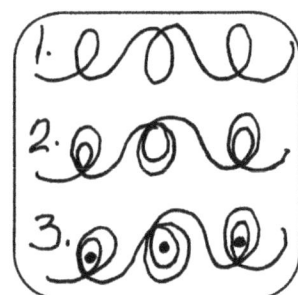

Dot & Dash

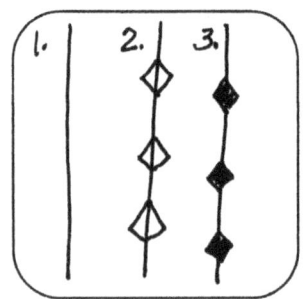 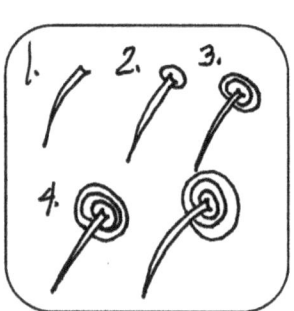 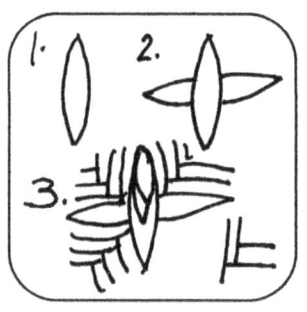 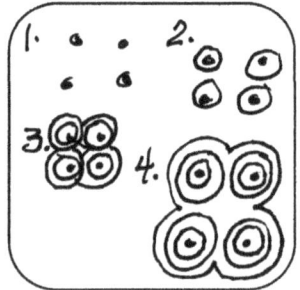

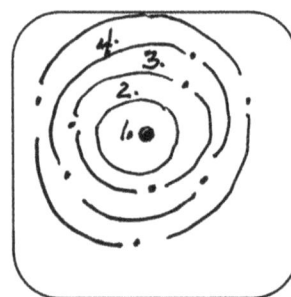 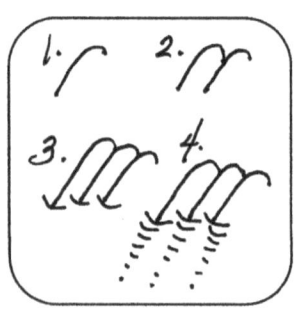 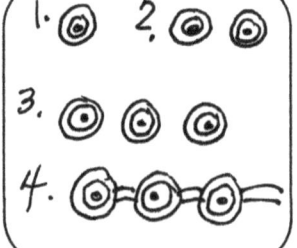 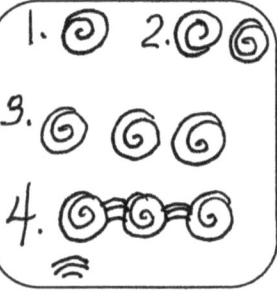

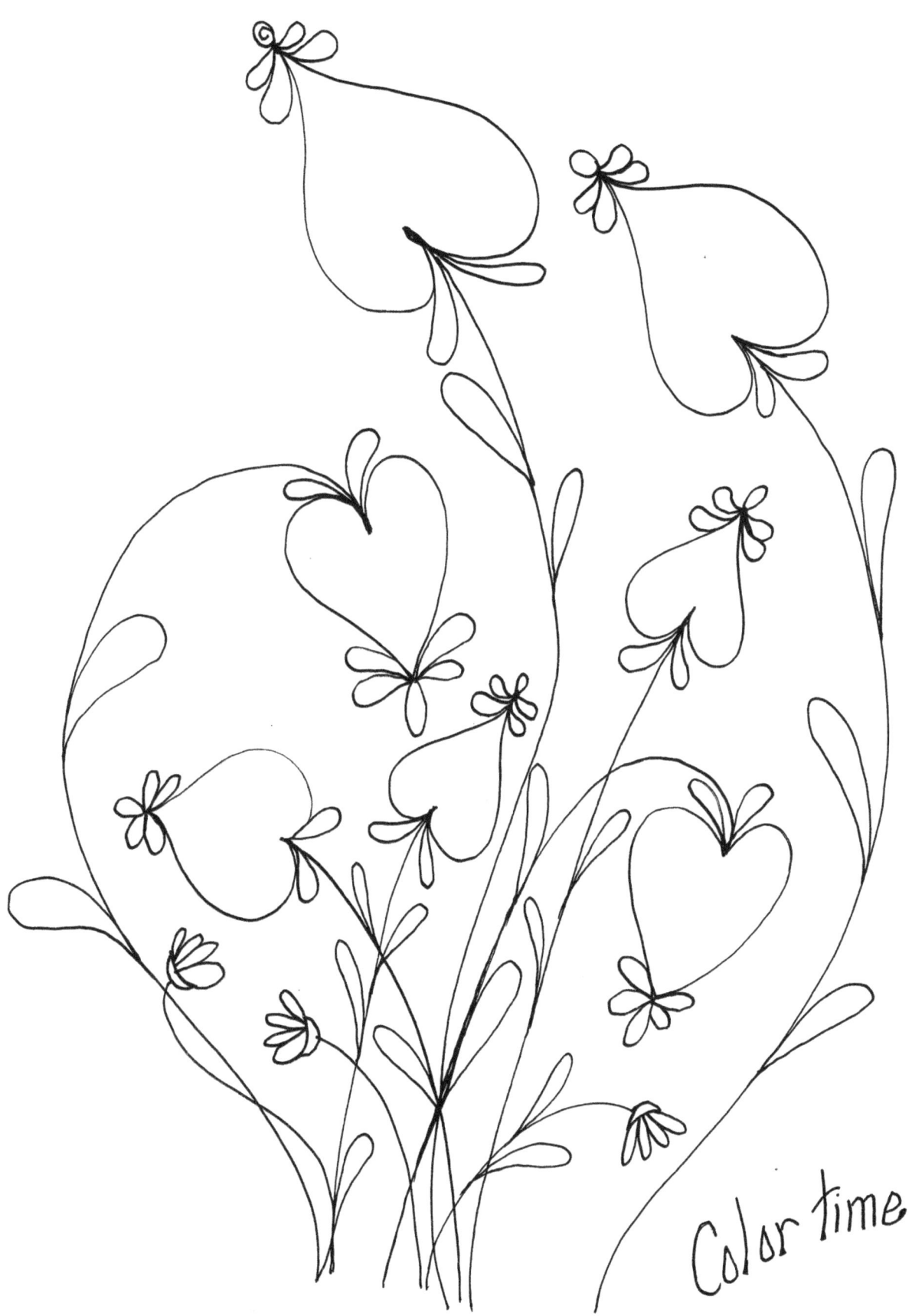

Color time

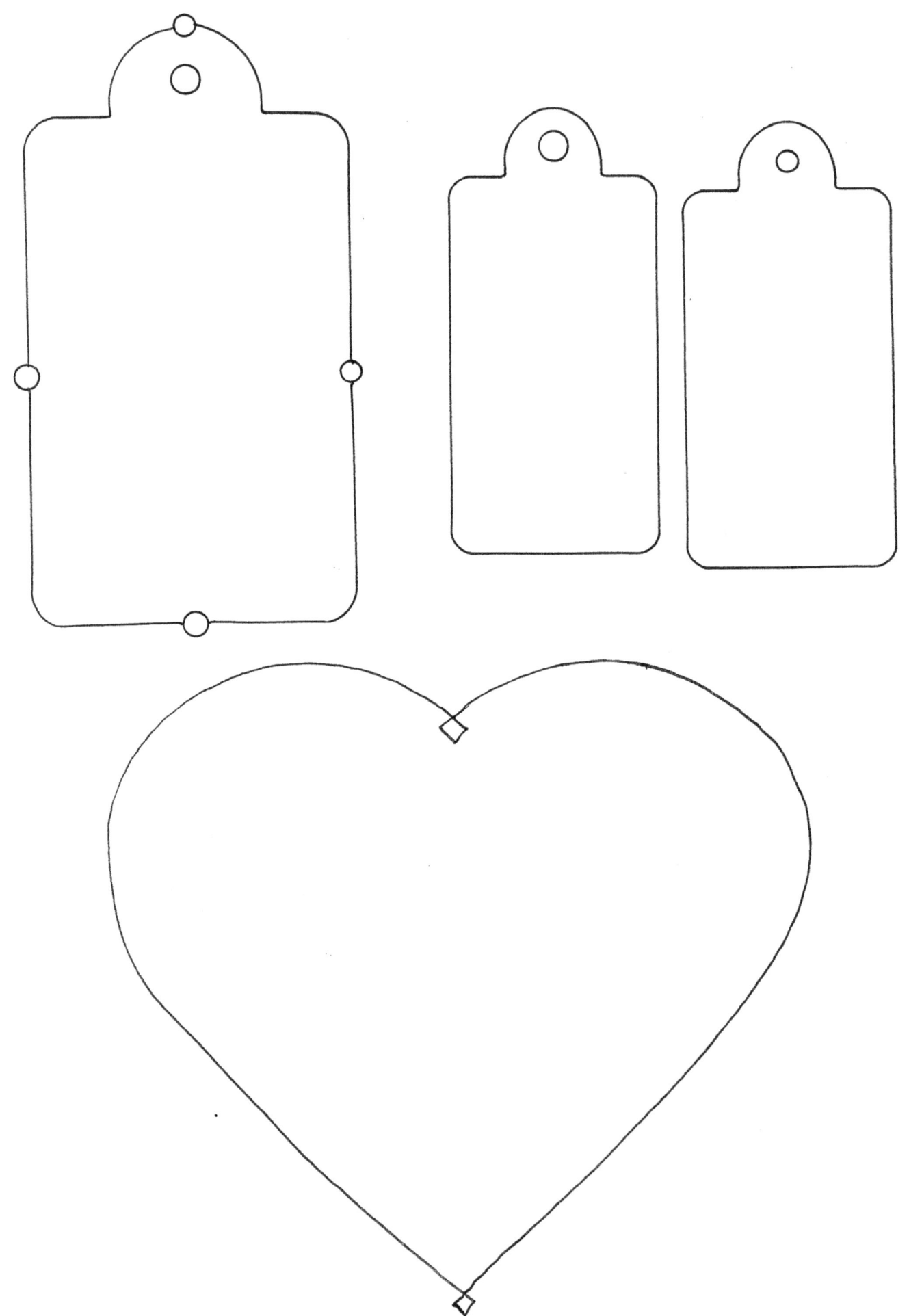

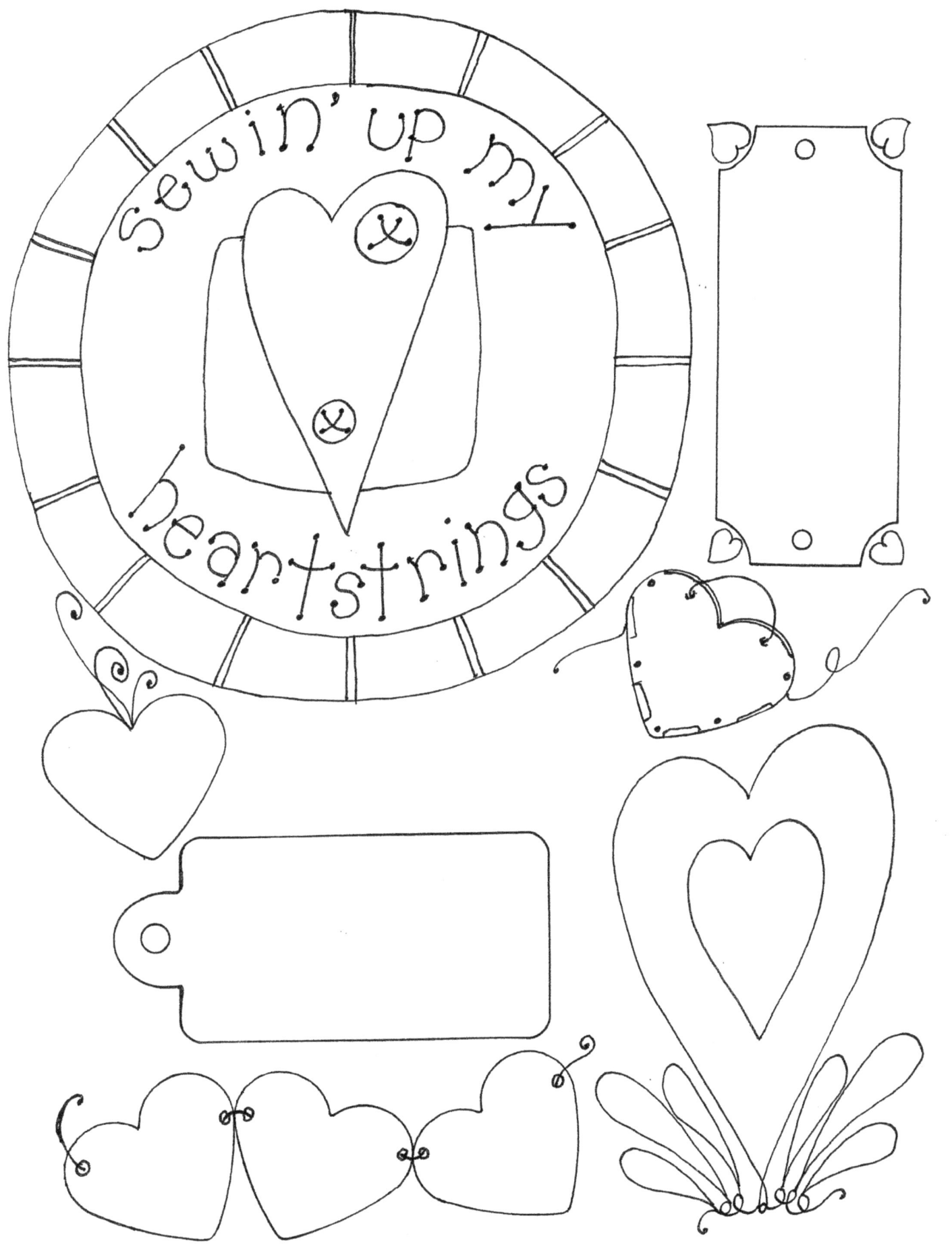

Sewin' up my heartstrings